CARAVAN
COOKBOOK

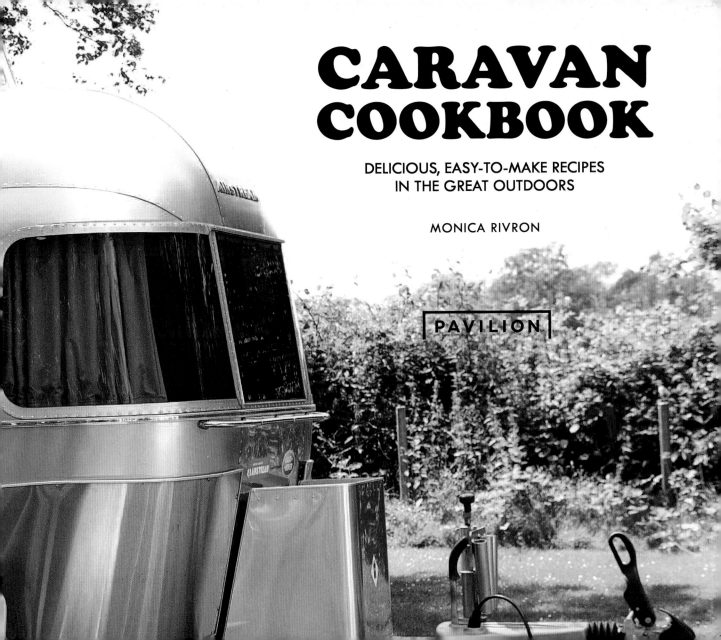

CARAVAN
COOKBOOK

DELICIOUS, EASY-TO-MAKE RECIPES IN THE GREAT OUTDOORS

Monica Rivron

PAVILION

contents

foreword

'Is it just me or does food taste better when you're outside …?'

I have a confession to make: the first time we set off on a caravanning holiday, we knew nothing. I didn't realise there were stabilisers on the back and front of a caravan – the funny little wheely thing near the towing bit seemed to be doing a fine job of keeping us on an even keel. And with perfectly good cafés and restaurants within a 15-mile radius of any site, it seemed madness to attempt to cook anything. The way I saw it, we were on holiday, and you don't wash up on holiday.

We really didn't get it first time out.

Of course, with the purchase of our first barbecue all that changed, and for a time pretty much anything slapped on the griddle worked for us. But to be honest, after a while, there's only so many ways to barbie a bit of chicken.

We were latecomers to caravanning and our introduction was somewhat unexpected. You could say we were press-ganged into it …

I'd been working on the BBC *Holiday* show for some time and out of the blue got a call asking if, for the next film, the family Rivron – that's myself, my wife Monica and the kids Dan, Ella and baby Ned – were up for a long weekend in the north of France. They were after a short film based round a do-it-yourself family break. This all sounded fine: the kids were of an age where pretty much anything is fun as long as it doesn't involve eating anything green, so why not …

I can't, or choose not to, remember my wife's exact words when the full realisation of the term 'do-it-yourself family break' dawned. The sticking point was the word 'caravan'. I can honestly say neither my wife nor I had ever had cause to use this word. Ever. The simple fact was that we just weren't vanners, our parents weren't vanners, their parents weren't vanners, and before that I'm fairly sure caravanning wasn't even a holiday option, certainly not if you lived in North London.

The plan was not only to tow a bloody great caravan to France but to holiday in it once we got there! Mad or what? The Caravan Club, fearing the worst, had thoughtfully made available a wooden cottage in the grounds of the campsite for the family to sleep in should the experience be too big a leap of faith.

Maybe I should point out here that, previous to this, the Rivron family's idea of a holiday was to board a plane just outside London, then eight or nine hours later arrive in Orlando, Florida, where we'd hand over all our money to a Mr M Mouse. Once we had done this, and it didn't take long, we'd board a plane in Orlando, Florida and finally arrive back in London. So I can put my hand on my heart and say that what happened on that historic trip in September 2000, at a campsite at La Bien Assise, a stone's throw from the northern coast of France, changed our lives for ever: we loved it.

This book is a collection of some of our favourite meals lovingly cooked by Monica and thoroughly enjoyed by all of us whilst caravanning. We hope you enjoy them too.

I think I should mention here that Monica's the trained chef, having studied under Pru Leith at her Cookery School. I'm very much not a trained chef but did get through to the second round of *Celebrity Masterchef*, so I do know one end of a knife from the other and can dice veg until the cows come home. And, truth be known, that's pretty much all I'm allowed to do ...

Over to you, Mon.

Rowland Rivron

introduction

Food is a huge part of a holiday for me. Many of my best memories are from around the table; we regularly find ourselves at the table well after midnight, chatting in the candlelight. What I enjoy is good, unpretentious food that the whole family can appreciate.

I also love shopping for the ingredients – whether it's from a local farm shop or a market. I even enjoy shopping in foreign supermarkets. My husband gets really impatient when I linger in the aisles, looking at the way things are packaged and labelled.

This book is a collection of our family favourites. Delicious, uncomplicated recipes that are simple and quick to prepare and that won't leave you feeling like you have spent your entire holiday slaving in a hot caravan. I have tried to keep the washing-up to a minimum and a careful eye on the gas bottle.

Now for a confession: I love rainy days in the caravan. It makes me feel really cosy, the whole family sheltering in our little holiday home. And that's when I reach for a mixing bowl and wooden spoon to knock up a cake or other treat.

All the recipes in this book have been tried, tested and refined for my family across many years of caravanning. All comprise simple, fresh ingredients that can be bought easily wherever you are. With husband Rowland, and a family of three children (Dan, Ella and Ned) ranging in age from 10 to 15, there's always a hungry tummy to fill. Hopefully you'll agree that this book provides some inspirational solutions.

Happy caravanning!

Monica

Monica R

don't leave home without these!

Of course you'll be plundering the local supermarkets, the campsite shop and, best of all, local markets for delicious produce, but there are a few store cupboard staples, aside from the essential tea, coffee and bottle of wine, that are useful to take with you if you have room …

'H' is for: Hellman's mayonnaise, Heinz tomato ketchup and HP sauce. You have to take them, you know you do! I also use a great deal of pesto in my recipes, partly because it's delicious and partly because crushed garlic gets everywhere and you don't want to be smelling it for the rest of your holiday. I have found it's sometimes hard to buy pesto in France, so just to be on the safe side I pack it in abundance. You can't beat pesto pasta for a first evening meal after setting up.

My other must-haves are teriyaki marinade and sukiyaki stir-fry sauce. Teriyaki is a wonderful marinade; it is a great way of tenderising chicken or beef and is perfect for barbecuing. Just place the beef or chicken in a dish and pour over the teriyaki, let the meat marinate all day or for as little as 30 minutes, depending on how much time you have, then cook the meat. As well as making the meat more tender, it provides a lovely subtle flavour (see my recipe for Five-Minute Stir-fry pages 66–7). Sukiyaki stir-fry sauce is perfect for fish. One of our staple meals is pan-fried coley. I just sprinkle a little sukiyaki sauce over the fish just before I pan-fry it in butter on the skillet pan. It is absolutely delicious.

For something sweet to keep you going, Dundee Cake (page 18) and Banana Bread (page 19) are fantastic cakes to take on a journey. They keep for days and are best made at home and then taken with, as both need quite a long cooking time. You can of course make them in your caravan, but remember not to run out of gas!

utensils

Here's a list of utensils I think you will need in your caravan kitchen. You have to be very careful not to over-pack but, on the other hand, having the right utensils makes all the difference.

I have found a slow cooker to be a very useful piece of equipment. It is a great way to cook stews and soups and even curries without using up precious gas. It also means you can come back to a wonderful dinner that has been cooking itself for as long as you've been out. See pages 82–91 for some delicious slow cooker recipes.

I am also a big fan of silicone cake tins. They don't need lining and greasing and they're very easy to wash up.

Pots and pans
- 3 saucepans (small, medium, large)
- 2 frying pans (small, large)
- skillet pan (a heavy, ridged frying pan)
- wok

Oven dishes
- casserole dish
- large roasting dish
- 2 baking trays
- tart dish
- 450g/1lb (24 x 10cm/9^1/2 x 4in) loaf tin
- 20cm (8in) round cake tin
- fairy (cup) cake tin
- cooling tray

Other equipment
- large mixing bowl
- 3 small mixing bowls
- small whisk
- garlic crusher
- pallet knife
- spatula
- cheese grater
- pastry brush
- scissors
- sharp knives (small, medium, large)
- chopping board
- 3 wooden spoons
- lemon squeezer
- slotted spoon
- colander

- sieve
- measuring jug
- rolling pin
- weighing scales
- tin opener
- vegetable peeler

Barbecue equipment
- large tongs
- wooden or metal skewers

Electrical equipment
- kettle
- handheld whisk
- handheld blender
- slow cooker

in the store cupboard

Essentials
- olive oil
- white wine vinegar
- dried pasta, rice and couscous
- flour (plain and self-raising)
- baking powder
- tomato purée
- pesto
- tomato and basil sauce (jar or carton)

Tins of...
- sweetcorn
- coconut milk
- chickpeas
- adzuki beans
- butter beans
- red kidney beans
- tuna

Seasonings
- stock cubes
- tabasco (Rowland's favourite!)
- Maggi liquid seasoning (another favourite)
- teriyaki marinade
- sukiyaki stir-fry sauce
- English mustard
- dried tarragon
- dried coriander
- ground cayenne
- cumin
- turmeric
- saffron
- tandoori curry powder

CHIPIRONES

en su tinta

LULAS
com tin

...s y Mariscos

Peña

...UIDS

n ink

BONITO DEL M...

ORTI...

EN ESCABE...

Pimentón de la...
Denominación de Origen...

SANTO DOM...

Calidad:
AGRIDULCE

1. FOOD ON THE GO

I love picnics. There is something really exciting about making up packages and reopening them in a lovely location. We have a sweet little picnic set that I bought in France and I have loads of very happy memories of using it.

The French have fantastic picnics, with tables and chairs, a table-cloth and disposable barbecue. One year Rowland, inspired by the French neighbours, lugged a set-up table across a blistering hot beach – never again! Ours is now a much more low-key affair with a rug.

I like using a plate when I'm on a picnic, and I am happy with a fork, but I think it is always a good idea to bring food that doesn't need a knife. Hummus and carrot sticks are a must: they travel well and if any little tummies start rumbling before you get to your picnic spot you can always pull them out. Sausage rolls (pages 20–1) are also great for handing round while you set up the picnic.

Cake is always a winner and can be made before you even leave home if you prefer. If you are picnicking on a beach or somewhere where there is a little café, consider buying your drinks, so they're nice and cold and the picnic bag is lighter.

dundee cake

You can make this cake a few days before you go, as it takes quite a long time to cook and it just gets better and better with time. It is very simple to make and it's a lovely holiday cake because it is light.

150g/5¹/₂oz/scant ³/₄ cup butter
150g/5¹/₂oz/scant ³/₄ cup caster sugar
3 eggs, beaten
225g/8oz/1¹/₂ cups plain flour, sifted
1 tsp baking powder
175g/6oz/generous 1¹/₄ cups currants
175g/6oz/1 cup sultanas
50g/1³/₄oz/scant ¹/₃ cup candied peel
juice of 1 orange
50g/1³/₄oz/generous ¹/₂ cup ground almonds
50g/1³/₄oz/ ¹/₃ cup whole blanched almonds

Preparation

Preheat the oven to 180°C/350°F/Gas mark 4. Grease and line an 18–20cm (7–8in) cake tin (or use a non-stick one).

Cream the butter and the sugar together, then add the eggs a little at a time. Fold in the flour and baking powder. Add the currants, sultanas, candied peel, orange juice and ground almonds. Tip the mixture into the cake tin and spread it evenly, then pop the whole almonds in a circle on the top of the cake; don't push them down too far, or they will sink. Bake in the centre of the oven.

Check the cake after 2 hours: gently press down and if it springs back, it is ready; if not, it needs a little longer. Cool and then pack in an airtight container.

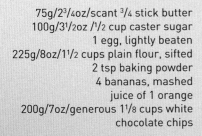

banana bread

This is a wonderful picnic cake, but is even better as a 'travel' cake. As it takes quite a long time to bake, I suggest you make it before you go and enjoy it on the way. A friend of ours, who was doing some decorating for us, once described it as 'a taste explosion in your mouth'!

75g/2³/₄oz/scant ³/₄ stick butter
100g/3¹/₂oz /¹/₂ cup caster sugar
1 egg, lightly beaten
225g/8oz/1¹/₂ cups plain flour, sifted
2 tsp baking powder
4 bananas, mashed
juice of 1 orange
200g/7oz/generous 1¹/₈ cups white chocolate chips

Preparation
Grease and line a loaf tin about 24 x 10cm (9¹/₂ x 4in). Preheat the oven to 180°C/350°F/Gas mark 4.

Cream the butter and the sugar, then beat in the egg. Tip in the flour and baking powder, and mix again; it will look very dry, but don't worry. Add the banana and the orange juice, then add the chocolate chips, giving the mixture one last mix. Pour into the tin and bake for 1 hour.

Check the bread is ready by making sure the centre springs back when you press down on it. Remove from the oven and leave in the tin for about 10 minutes, then turn out onto a cooling tray.

Make sure that you put this into an airtight container for your travels only after it has completely cooled.

sausage, leek and mozzarella rolls

These rolls keep and travel well in an air-tight container, making them the ideal hearty snack if you are heading off to the beach or on a hike somewhere. They can also be heated up and served with some salad and pickles. We always try and have some on the go, as they provide the perfect alternative to sweet things when the kids nag between meals.

Once you've made these a few times, you'll find yourself experimenting with ingredients. Rowland likes his with a bit of a kick, so a few splashes of Tabasco sauce or chilli oil in the mix works wonders and also warms the cockles

Use ready-made puff pastry – you're on holiday after all!

Preparation

Preheat the oven to 220°C/425°F/Gas mark 7.

Squeeze the sausage meat out of the skins into your mixing bowl. (If you've got kids, get them to do this bit; they love it.) Add the mozzarella to the sausage meat.

In a large frying pan, sauté the onions till they are opaque or glassy-looking, then add the leek. Turn over in the pan once and add the water, which will gently cook the leeks. When the water has evaporated, the leeks will be cooked but not dried out.

Makes 8

6 large pork sausages, total weight about 350g/12oz
150g/5½oz mozzarella cheese, chopped into cubes
2 onions, chopped into cubes
2 leeks, chopped into cubes
200ml/7fl oz/generous ¾ cup water
1 small bunch fresh parsley, finely chopped
375g/13oz puff pastry
1 large or 2 small eggs, beaten
salt and pepper
flour, for rolling

Transfer the onions and leeks into the bowl with the sausage and mozzarella, season with salt and pepper and mix thoroughly. You can do this with a spoon, but I find it's much better getting your hands dirty at this point. Add the chopped parsley, then mix until all the ingredients are evenly blended together. Put to one side.

Sprinkle some flour onto the counter top and flour your rolling pin so that nothing sticks. Roll out your pastry, making sure you don't go too thin. You want to end up with a large rectangle that can be scored down the middle to create two oblong strips.

Arrange the mix in a chunky thick line down the long side of each pastry strip. (Convention says you should roll the mix with floured hands into a long sausage; if you do this, try not to let it get too thin). Paint some of the whisked egg along the pastry opposite the mix – this will act as a glue to stop the rolls unfolding when cooking. Roll the mix into the pastry towards the egg.

Cut each pastry roll into four and glaze with the remaining egg. Place the eight rolls on a baking tray and cook for 25 minutes, or until golden brown.

squashed french bread sandwich

This sounds really strange but it is absolutely delicious. I generally make these when we are going to the beach.

For each sandwich, you want about one-third of one of the fatter French sticks.

iceberg lettuce, sliced
pesto
gruyère or jarlsberg cheese
ham slices
mayonnaise

Preparation
Cut the bread though the middle and spread 1 teaspoon pesto on both sides instead of butter. On one half, put a thin slice of gruyère or jarlsberg cheese (I slice the cheese with the vegetable peeler) and then a thin slice of ham. Spread 1 teaspoon mayonnaise and then pile on the lettuce. Sandwich the bread together and cover in clingfilm tightly. When it's securely wrapped, pushed down quite heavily with the palm of your hand. This makes the pesto ooze into the bread and squishes all the ingredients together, which makes for the most amazing sandwich sensation!

vegetarian pasties

These are wonderful and so versatile. You can serve them warm with a salad lunch, pack them and take them with you on a picnic. I use readymade prepared shortcrust pastry, and beat the egg in a jam jar, keeping any leftover in the fridge.

Makes 6
1 mozzarella, cut into cubes
100g/3¹/₂oz/2 cups button mushrooms, sliced
2 leeks, sliced into small pieces
1 sweet red pepper, chopped finely
500g/1lb 2oz shortcrust pastry
1 egg, beaten
butter for frying

Preparation
Preheat the oven to 200°C/400°F/Gas mark 6.
   Put the mozzarella cheese into a mixing bowl.
   In a frying pan melt the butter and then add the mushrooms, leeks and peppers. Turn the mixture over all the time and take off the heat when the mushrooms look cooked. Tip them into the mixing bowl with the cheese and mix with a wooden spoon until the cheese is all mixed in, then season with salt and pepper.
   Roll out the pastry to the thickness of a £2 coin. Cut the pastry into six circles (each about the size of a small side plate). Divide the filling evenly between the circles, putting the mixture in the middle. Paint the outer rim of the circle with egg and pull edges of the circle up to meet and stick together at the top, making a ridge that runs the length of the pasty.
   Cook for approximately 20 minutes or until golden brown.

coronation chicken

This is such a useful dish, I simply had to include it. And, let's face it – it's everyone's guilty secret. You can serve this as a main dish with rice, or use it as a sandwich filler. You can even take it on a picnic; it works every time.

Serves 4
4 chicken breasts
200ml/7fl oz/generous 3/4 cup water
1 onion, chopped
100ml/3¹/2fl oz/scant 1/2 cup white wine
1 tbsp mild curry powder
1 tbsp apricot jam
4 tbsp mayonnaise
50ml/2fl oz/scant 1/4 cup double cream
50g/1³/4oz/1/3 cup chopped walnuts
1 tbsp parsley, chopped

Preparation
Preheat the oven to 180°C/350°F/Gas mark 4.
  Put the chicken breasts in an ovenproof dish and pour over the water, then bake for 20 minutes. When cooked, leave to cool, cut into small pieces and place in your mixing bowl. (Alternatively, if you're in a hurry, you can use ready-cooked chicken breast.)
  To make the sauce, sauté the onion, then add the white wine and curry powder. Cook for 3 minutes, then tip into the chicken bowl. Add the apricot jam, mayonnaise, double cream, walnuts and parsley and fold in the mixture.
  Serve as you wish!

rivron rice

This is named Rivron Rice because I make this all the time when we are in the caravan. It is so versatile: you can pack it in a picnic, serve it with barbecued food or just serve it as a light lunch dish. I always measure rice in a jug; I find it much easier. I reckon about 100ml/$3^1/_2$fl oz/scant $^1/_2$ cup per person.

Serves 4
400ml/14fl oz/scant 2 cups rice
4 ham slices, cut into small pieces
285g/10oz canned sweetcorn
100g/$3^1/_2$oz/2 cups button mushrooms, sliced
1 tsp cumin
50g/$1^3/_4$oz/$^1/_3$ cup pine nuts
butter and olive oil, for frying

Preparation
Cook the rice: make sure you fill the pan with at least double the amount of water and bring to the boil, then simmer for about 12 minutes; as soon as you smell that rice smell, you know it is cooked. Pour out into a sieve and shake out any excess water, then tip into a large bowl. Add the ham and the sweetcorn.

In a small frying pan, melt a knob of butter, then cook the mushrooms till golden brown. Add them to the rice. In the same frying pan, heat a tiny amount of olive oil, then add the cumin. When sizzling, add the pine nuts and cook for a few minutes till golden brown; don't take your eyes off them because they turn from golden to burned in the blink of an eye. Add the pine nuts to your rice salad and stir all the ingredients.

You can serve this salad immediately warm, or you can make it in advance and serve it cold.

chicken satay

Pick this recipe when you have plenty of time to enjoy making the different aspects of this dish: the marinade for the chicken and the satay sauce. I have my beautiful assistant Rowland, who is an expert at chopping; he is kept very busy when we decide to have chicken satay! The satay sauce can be prepared in advance. (If you don't want to make the satay, the chicken is also delicious in a pitta bread sandwich with some hummus and salad.)

Preparation
Put the chicken in a bowl with the sherry, soy sauce, ginger and garlic and leave to marinate for at least 1 hour – and longer if possible.

   Chop the shallots, ginger and garlic from the sauce into tiny cubes – small as you can. Slice the chillies in half and remove the seeds and inner pith, then chop the chilli small as you can. Squeeze the lime.

   Soak the wooden skewers in water; this stops them from burning when you cook the chicken.

Serves 4
4 chicken breasts – boned and skinned, then sliced thinly
Marinade
100ml/3½fl oz/scant ½ cup medium sherry
2 tbsp soy sauce
3cm/1¼in piece of ginger, cut into cubes
6 garlic cloves, cut into cubes
Satay Sauce
2 shallots
2cm/¾in cube of ginger
2 garlic cloves
2 red chillies
juice of ½ lime
150g/5½oz/scant ¾ cup coarse peanut butter
1 tsp soft brown sugar
about 3 tbsp water
wooden skewers

You are now ready to start. In a frying pan, sauté the shallots. (I use sesame oil, but you can use olive oil.) After about 1 minute, add the chillies, ginger and garlic and cook for a further 2 minutes, taking care to stir all time, to prevent burning. Add the lime, peanut butter, sugar and water and turn over in the pan until every thing has blended. You should get a really fantastic smell. Your satay sauce is ready! Put it into a little serving dish and set aside.

When you are ready to cook the chicken, take it out of the marinade and thread onto skewers. I tend to fold the chicken so that the skewer runs through each piece twice, keeping it secure. Brush off any excess ginger or garlic with a pastry brush.

In a skillet pan, heat a mixture of olive oil and nut oil, then cook the chicken; you will be able to tell easily when it is cooked, as it has a lovely golden brown colour.

Serve immediately.

spicy couscous salad

This is, as it says, spicy. If you are not keen on spices, just reduce the amount of chilli flakes or take out altogether.

Serves 4
200g/7oz/1 cup couscous
250ml/9fl oz/1 cup chicken stock, made from a stock cube
1 sweet red pepper
6cm/2$\frac{1}{2}$in piece of cucumber
8 small or 4 large spring onions, finely sliced
50g/1$\frac{3}{4}$oz/ $\frac{1}{3}$ cup pine nuts
1 tsp chilli flakes
6 mint leaves, finely chopped
6 basil leaves, finely chopped
butter, and olive oil for frying

Preparation
Put the couscous in a large mixing bowl and pour the stock over the couscous, then add a knob of butter. Mix the couscous and allow the stock to be absorbed. When cool, fluff it up by gently folding the couscous with a fork.

Deseed the red pepper and slice into little bits, then chop the cucumber up into tiny little bits (smaller than the pepper).

Heat a small amount of oil in the frying pan and gently fry the sweet red pepper. After 2–3 minutes, add the pine nuts and chilli flakes to the pan and continue cooking. Watch the pine nuts, they burn really easily; as soon as they start to go golden, take them off the heat and tip the entire contents of the pan into the couscous. Mix well with a fork. Finally, add the cucumber, spring onions and mint and basil leaves. This salad tastes better if it is left for a while. Store in an airtight container.

falafel

These are fantastic for picnics: very quick to prepare and can be made the day before and stored in an airtight container.

Makes 12
400g/14oz canned chickpeas
1 onion, finely chopped
4 garlic cloves, crushed
3 tsp tahini
1 tsp coriander
1 tsp turmeric
1 tsp cumin
large pinch salt
2 tbsp plain flour, sifted
olive oil for frying

Preparation
In a mixing bowl put the chickpeas, onion, garlic, tahini, spices and salt. Using a strong fork, mash all the ingredients together until they are well crushed and blended together. Flour your hands and make little balls – this mixture should make 12 falafel. Put each ball between your two palms and flatten slightly; this shape is easier for shallow-frying.

Pour just less than 1cm/$\frac{1}{2}$in of olive oil into your pan, and heat. When it is sizzling, add all the falafel and fry; they will take about 2 minutes each side. Take out and drain on absorbent kitchen paper.

Serve warm or cold.

parma ham and peach salad

This is the perfect salad for a beautiful summer day and can be served as light lunch or as a side dish.

Serves 4
lettuce (use a delicate leaf such as lamb's lettuce or rocket leaves rather than iceberg)
3 peaches
6 slices of Parma ham
1 mozzarella
6 mint leaves

Preparation
Slice the peaches in half and stone them, then slice each half into about 4 or 5 pieces. Slice or tear the mozzarella, first in half, and then each half into about 6 or 8 slices. Tear up the Parma ham into little bite size pieces. Using scissors, chop up the mint finely. Wash and shred the lettuce. Line your serving dish with the lettuce, then put the rest of the salad into the dish and gently toss. This salad is so flavoursome you don't need to dress it, just serve as is.

tuna and butterbean mayonnaise

This is a really lovely light cold lunch dish to serve on a hot day, and you can always take it on a picnic too.

Serves 4
200g/7oz canned tuna
300g/10oz canned butterbeans
2 tbsp mayonnaise
3 spring onions, chopped small
$1/2$ sweet red pepper, finely sliced
1 tbsp chopped parsley, finely chopped

Preparation
Put all the ingredients into a bowl and stir until it is all nicely mixed in together.

potato and bacon salad

This is a meal in itself and a must for any picnic. I always make double the amount; it is so useful to have in the fridge and will keep for a few days.

Serves 4
700g/1lb 9oz new potatoes
250g/9oz bacon, cut into the size of small croutons
10 spring onions, sliced
2 tbsp French dressing (see below)
2 tsbp chopped coriander
2 tbsp mayonnaise

French Dressing
1 tsp Dijon mustard
pinch of sugar
1 tbsp white or red wine vinegar
salt and pepper
6 tbsp extra-virgin olive oil

Preparation
Make the French Dressing by whisking the mustard, sugar, vinegar and seasoning together in a bowl. Now gradually whisk in the olive oil until thickened (or put all the ingredients in a screw-top jar and shake well!).

Cut the potatoes in half if they are small new potatoes or quarters if they are large; you want fairly small pieces. Put the potatoes on the boil in salted water. While they are cooking, fry the bacon. When it is almost ready, add the spring onion; make sure the bacon is well cooked, almost crispy. Put the bacon and onions into your large mixing bowl. When the potatoes are really well cooked, splitting the skins, drain and tip into the mixing bowl. Add the French Dressing and turn the mixture around so all the potatoes are covered in dressing and the bacon. Leave to one side and when cool add the mayonnaise and coriander and fold in carefully to make sure it is all thoroughly mixed.

2. LIGHT SNACKS & SALADS

If we are spending the day on the campsite, I really enjoy lunch. If the sun is shining and all the camp jobs are done, you can put up the sun umbrella and lay the table outside for a leisurely lunch … We usually have two or three dishes and Rowland makes a salad – there is nothing better than assembling a dish using lovely fresh produce you have come across if you have been to a market in the morning. If we have bought a melon, it has to be melon and Parma ham.

I always keep some Tuna and Butterbean Mayonnaise (page 32) in the fridge because the children always arrive back from the pool, dripping wet, and announce they are starving – a tuna baguette is the perfect quick fix!

the too busy salad

This is a salad that my husband Rowland devised and I named. I prefer my salads quite simple but Rowland has a tendency to overdo it with the amount of ingredients he uses. This one does actually work and, I have to admit, is almost a meal in itself.

Serves 4
¼ of an iceberg lettuce
handful of rocket
few sprigs of watercress
1 stick of celery
6 thick slices of cucumber, quartered
6– 8 plum tomatoes, halved
3 spring onions
nuts, a handful
cumin seeds or powder
oil

Preparation
Roughly shred the iceberg lettuce and place in the salad bowl, then mix in the rocket leaves and watercress. Chop up the celery and cucumber, and halve the tomatoes, then add all to the salad. Finely slice the spring onions lengthwise into long thin shards (rather than small rings) and put to one side.

Now dice up your nuts – the more varieties the better.

If you are using cumin seeds, sprinkle these into a small frying pan and heat through, taking care not to burn them. Then tip the seeds onto a hard surface and roll a jam jar, or similar, over them to crush them. (I'm assuming here your caravan is not equipped with a pestle and mortar; ours isn't …)

In the same pan, pour in a little oil and heat. Tip the nuts in and then sift over the crushed cumin (sifting so that none of the cumin husks get involved). Alternatively, add the cumin powder. Heat through until the nuts turn a darker brown.

Pour the hot nuts in oil over the salad and then scatter the spring onions over the whole thing.

This salad and a slice of Leek and Mushroom Tart (page 47) is a perfect compromise between a snack and a full meal.

This is a lovely, gentle recipe. If you've had lots of rich food and fancy something light, this is the one for you.

rolled ham with leeks

Makes 10

10 leeks
50g/1³⁄₄oz/scant ¹⁄₄ cup butter
50g/1³⁄₄oz/ ¹⁄₃ cup plain flour
400ml/14fl oz/scant 1³⁄₄ cups milk
100g/3¹⁄₂oz/1 cup cheddar cheese, grated
¹⁄₂ tsp cayenne pepper
10 slices of honey roast ham
1 handful breadcrumbs

Preparation

Preheat the oven to 200°C/400°F/Gas mark 6.

Top and tail the leeks; if the outer skin looks tough, take it off. Bring a pan of water to the boil and cook the leeks for 5 minutes in the water.

Meanwhile, make the cheese sauce by melting the butter in a pan. When the butter is sizzling, add the flour and stir into a paste. Take off the heat and add the milk, then return to the heat and stir continuously. When the sauce is smooth, add the cheese and cayenne pepper, then gently bring up to a simmer for 2 minutes, or until all the cheese is melted.

Roll a piece of ham around each leek and put them into an ovenproof dish, pour the cheese sauce on top and sprinkle with breadcrumbs. Cook in the oven for 20 minutes.

Serve with a green salad.

tomato and basil tart

There's something wonderful about serving up a home-made tart. This one tastes delicious and is full of beautiful summer ingredients. Some locally produced mozzarella or similar soft cheese will make it taste even more authentic. I recommend using scissors to chop basil rather than a knife, which bruises the leaves.

Serves 4
200g/7oz cherry tomatoes
375g/13oz puff pastry
2 tbsp pesto
250g/9oz mozzarella cheese, cut into cubes
5 basil leaves
handful rocket leaves

Preparation

Preheat the oven to 180°C/350°F/Gas mark 4. Paint your baking tray with oil.

Slice the tomatoes in half around the equator.

Roll out the pastry so it fits nicely into your baking tray. Dab the pesto onto the pastry, keeping clear a 2cm/¾in edge all the way round. Cover the pesto with a layer of cherry tomatoes, leaving tiny gaps in between so the cheese can ooze in, and place mozzarella cheese on top, leaving gaps to avoid a solid layer of cheese. Bake for 20 minutes.

Transfer the tart to a serving dish, taking care because this is a delicate dish, then sprinkle over the basil and rocket leaves.

Serve warm.

moules marinières

Don't be scared: all you need is a very large pan. It is so easy to prepare and if you are staying anywhere near the sea you are likely to come across a fishmonger selling lovely fresh mussels.

I get one of the kids to scooter up to the campsite café to buy portions of *pommes frites* to go with the *moules*. It's one of the meals I most look forward to; I find it really difficult to eat *moules* if we're not in the caravan.

I reckon on using 500g/1lb 2oz mussels per person.

Serves 4
2kg/4lb 8oz mussels
2 onions, chopped
2 celery sticks, chopped
3 garlic cloves, crushed
50g/1^3/4oz/scant ^{1}/2 stick butter
a dash of olive oil
200ml/7fl oz/generous ^{3}/4 cup white wine
200ml/7fl oz/generous ^{3}/4 cup water
220ml/8fl oz/scant 1 cup double cream
2 tbsp chopped parsley

Preparation
Clean the mussels by scrubbing them under a running tap. Pull away any hairy bits and throw away any mussels that are cracked.
   In a large pan, simmer the onion, celery and garlic in the butter and oil for about 2 minutes, then add the wine and water and bring up to the boil. Tip in the mussels, put a lid on the pan and steam the mussels over a gentle heat, occasionally shaking the pan, until all the mussels open. This should take 5–6 minutes. Pour the mussels into a colander over a large mixing bowl to keep the liquid. Throw away any mussels that have not opened.
   Pour the liquid into a saucepan and stir in the double cream; bring up to a gentle simmer and season.
   Serve the mussels in big bowls, pouring over the liquid and sprinkling with parsley.
   Make sure you have bread to soak up the delicious juices.

fried calamari rings

A dish that is often enjoyed in restaurants but rarely attempted at home. The calamari are best fried in a wok, but you could use a large pan.

I always buy the squid washed and gutted: it's a palaver to do it yourself!

Serves 4
600g/1lb 5oz squid
100g/3^1/$_2$oz/ ^{2}/$_3$ cup plain flour
^{1}/$_2$ tsp cayenne pepper
^{1}/$_2$ tsp paprika
1 egg
300ml/10fl oz/1^1/$_4$ cups olive oil

Preparation
Slice the squid into rings about 1cm/^{1}/$_2$in thick. Sift the flour with the cayenne pepper and paprika into two mixing bowls. In another small bowl, beat the egg. Put some absorbent kitchen paper on a plate.

Put the squid in one of the flour bowls and shake the bowl to make sure each ring is covered in flour. Dip into the egg and then pop into the second bowl of flour. Heat the oil in the wok; when it is sizzling, add the first batch of squid rings, using a slotted spoon to separate any that have stuck together. Meanwhile, dip another batch of squid rings in the egg and flour. When the first batch is a golden brown, drain on the absorbent kitchen paper and cook the second batch. Repeat the process until all the squid rings are cooked. This should take no longer than 10 minutes.

Tip them into your serving dish, sprinkle liberally with salt and serve with lemon wedges and mayonnaise.

sweet chilli prawns

If you are holidaying by the sea, it is always nice to serve seafood. This prawn recipe is very simple to prepare. It was inspired by many visits to La Plancha, a beautiful seafood restaurant right on the beach, a little way down the coast from Biarritz.

Serves 4
juice of ¹/₂ lemon
4 garlic cloves, crushed
1 tbsp butter
1 tsp sugar
pinch chilli flakes
300g/10¹/₂oz king prawns, cooked and peeled

Preparation
Put the lemon, garlic, butter, sugar and chilli flakes in a wok or a large frying pan and heat gently to melt the butter and dissolve the sugar. Turn up the heat and add the prawns, and keep them turning over all the time. You are simply bringing the prawns up to a nice hot temperature, so this won't take long, 3–4 minutes depending on their size.

Serve immediately, spooning the juices over the prawns. They are delicious served with rice and a green salad.

prawn and rocket risotto

This is a wonderful dish if you are feeding a crowd. It uses only one pot, and you can serve it on a plate or in a bowl; it is absolutely delicious!

I prefer to use relatively large prawns.

Serves 4
50g/1³/4oz/scant ¼ cup butter
2 onions, finely chopped
1 celery stick, finely chopped
3 leeks, finely chopped
500g/1lb 2oz/2¹/3 cups Arborio rice
300ml/10fl oz/1¹/4 cups white wine
1 litre/1³/4 pints/4 cups stock
   (made from a stock cube will do)
200g/7oz prawns
60g/2¹/4oz wild rocket, chopped quite fine

Preparation
In your large saucepan, melt the butter, then add the onions and celery, stirring them to prevent them from burning. Add the leeks and the rice and turn the rice around in the pan to make sure all the rice gets covered with butter. Add the wine and stir well until it has evaporated.

Pour in a little of the stock in at a time and let that absorb into the rice, then add a little more. You cannot take your eyes of the pan and you must stir continually; otherwise, it will stick to the bottom of the pan. The whole process should take about 20 minutes. If your rice is still a little crunchy in the middle and you have used all your stock, add a small amount of water and keep simmering until the rice is soft and creamy. Add the prawns and rocket and keep on the heat for a further 2 minutes, stirring continuously. Then take off the heat and put the lid on and leave to settle for a few minutes. Serve immediately.

leek and mushroom tart

There's something incredibly satisfying about buying local fresh vegetables and enjoying them that same day. This is the perfect way to do it. The recipe is particularly lovely if you use different types of mushroom; white and chestnut, for example.

3 eggs
200ml/7fl oz/generous ¾ cup double cream
10 sheets filo pastry
2 onions, chopped
2 leeks, chopped into 3cm/1¼in strips
4 garlic bulbs, crushed
300g/10½oz mushrooms, sliced
100g/3½oz strong-flavoured hard cheese
    (such as Cheddar, Red Leicester or
    Double Gloucester), grated
olive oil

Preparation

Preheat the oven to 200°C/400°F/Gas mark 6.
   Whisk the eggs in your large mixing bowl and add the double cream. Brush a little olive oil around a tart dish, about 24cm/9½in round.
   Line the tart dish with the filo pastry. Use 2 sheets at a time, and lay the sheets across the dish so the corners of the pastry are sticking up. Space the filo sheets at regular intervals all around the dish so that it looks like a sunflower. Brush the pastry with oil and pop in the oven for about 5 minutes. Be careful; it can burn really easily.
   Sauté your onions in a large frying pan for about 1 minute. When glassy, add the leeks and garlic, stirring all the time until the leeks have softened. Add the mushrooms and stir until they are golden brown. Take off the heat and tip the mixture into the egg/cream mix and gently stir in the grated cheese.
   Pour the mixture into your filo-lined tart dish and pop back in the oven for 25 minutes or until the tart has set. Check after 20 minutes; you don't want it overcooked, and it's gorgeous if you catch it just set!
   Delicious hot or cold with salad.

... TO MARKET, TO MARKET

Food shopping on holiday can be a complete pleasure and also the source of much fresh 'instant food' for picnics and quick lunches. My favourite past-time has to be shopping in small villages and markets, but even the biggest super-market will probably stock a good selection of local fruit and vegetables. Try and find out when local markets are running and seek out local shops and farmers' co-operatives to get a real flavour of the region where you're staying. In Spain, the local *mercado* will have stalls stocking fine local oils, vinegars, cheeses and meats that are peculiar to the region, many of which are rarely exported out of the country.

Cheese-buying is always high on our shopping agenda and we have great fun deciding what we're going to buy. The great thing about buying cheese from local markets is the opportunity to 'try before you buy' – stallholders are usually more than happy for you to taste anything you like the look of and some of the curious ones you don't. My all time favourite cheese has to be Le Roi des Fromages (King of Cheeses) *Brie de Meaux*. It's at its best when it's just starting to ooze, or run, and is a meal in itself eaten with a roughly torn fresh crusty baguette and a bottle of fruity red wine, made from local grapes of course!

Look out for the little pots of jelly that go with cheese. In France they like the port-wine based gelée de porto, which is absolutely delicious. I always bring some home, as it's a perfect reminder of our holidays and one of the few food items that does travel well. In Spain, cheese is eaten with *membrillo casero*, a quince jelly, or a tomato jelly that has an intense flavour – the perfect accompaniment to a dry cheese. In most areas there will be locally produced variations of familiar favourites, such as mozzarella and Brie, so it's always worth experimenting to find something new that you like.

Locally produced meats make the perfect instant lunch. Chorizo can be a bit of a minefield since local producers often compete to produce the hottest variety, but it's a versatile 'must-have'. Serve it sliced as a little side dish, take it with you on a picnic or even put it on top of a pizza. If you come across some local air-dried ham such as Parma or Serrano, try a delicious Parma Ham and Peach Salad (page 31), or for a simple dish that just sums up summer, just a plate of melon and Parma ham. Use Cantaloupe melon if you can find it – the rich sweet flavour of goes really well with the salty ham.

I always buy local fruit and vegetables wherever possible. A few rich firm tomatoes, some fresh cucumber and you have the basics for a lovely Greek salad. Feta cheese is very easy to find in most local supermarkets; cut the cheese into little chunks, slice up a red onion and a red pepper. Add some black olives, sprinkle with a little oregano and you have a lovely salad – one of the best accompaniments for a barbecue.

Beautiful juicy oranges are the perfect picnic fruit – they travel well, are delicious freshly squeezed and can be used to make my Sugared

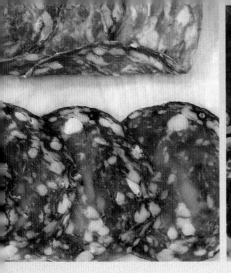

Oranges recipe (page 138). If you happen to come across some fresh raspberries, you can't beat raspberries and mascarpone. Take care when washing the raspberries: I put them in a little bowl of cold water and very gently stir the water, then dry them on kitchen roll, because the disintegrate so easily. Put the raspberries in a serving dish and sprinkle with caster sugar about an hour before serving and you will have a lovely rich syrup, then serve with a little dollop of mascarpone or Yogurt Cream (page 139). While we are on the subject of soft fruit, my Lemon Cream (page 135) goes beautifully with strawberries.

When I'm shopping on holiday I'm always on the look out for interesting looking tins, jars and labels. I have a 'thing' about packaging! I love bringing home my travel trophies and for the first few weeks after we return, using foreign packets is a gentle way of easing us back into the treadmill of home life post holiday. Seeing these packets on the shelves is a great reminder of carefree holidays in the caravan. One summer I bought a small box of individually wrapped sugar cubes with glamorous fifties-style models on the wrappers and I think we were still enjoying them the following Christmas …

bacon and scallop salad

This is a real holiday dish. I serve it with a big bowl of French fries from the campsite café. My son Ned acquired his taste for scallops while we were visiting a friend's restaurant. Ned was determined to try everything because he'd decided on his career path: skateboarding restaurant critic. Afterwards, I devised this simple salad using scallops, which we could all enjoy.

I suggest using 20 scallops. That may not sound a lot, but scallops are very filling.

Serves 4
200g/7oz spinach, shredded into strips 1cm/¹/₂in wide
4 bacon rashers, cut into tiny squares
100g/3¹/₂oz/2 cups button mushrooms, sliced
¹/₂ sweet red pepper, cut into matchsticks
20 scallops
4 garlic cloves, crushed
olive oil and butter, for frying

Preparation
Put the spinach onto your serving dish and put to one side. Pour a glug of olive oil in your large frying pan, and when it is sizzling tip in all the bacon. After 2 minutes, add the mushrooms and red pepper and continue to cook, turning all the time. When the bacon and mushrooms are well cooked, tip out onto the spinach.

Add a little more oil to the pan and an equal amount of butter. When the butter has melted, carefully cook the scallops. Turn the scallops over and then add the crushed garlic. The scallops will not take long to cook; about 2 minutes each side.

Carefully tip the scallops and the cooking juice onto the spinach. Use a spoon and fork to toss the salad. Serve immediately with Garlic Mayonnaise (see page 94).

tomato and bacon soup

This soup is a real standby for me. You can buy all the ingredients in the smallest of grocery shops, even the campsite shop. It's a delicious fresh soup that takes no time at all to prepare.

Serves 4
250g/9oz bacon, cut into small pieces
2 onions, chopped
10 tomatoes, chopped
700ml/1¼ pints/3 cups chicken stock, made with 1 stock cube
    (otherwise it will be too salty)
drizzle of double cream
1 tbsp coriander, finely chopped
olive oil

Preparation
In a large saucepan, gently cook the bacon in olive oil for 2 minutes. Add the onion and continue to cook until the onions look glassy and the bacon smells cooked. Add the chopped tomatoes and gently stir the mixture to make sure nothing sticks to the pan. When the tomatoes start to soften (about 3 minutes), take off the heat and add the stock.

Use a handheld blender to blend the soup until smooth. When you are ready to serve, put the soup back on the hob and bring it up to a very gentle simmer; never boil soup, because you lose all the flavour. Add a drizzle of double cream and sprinkle over coriander.

Serve with bread.

rivron deep-pan omelette

This is a great brunch dish, but also makes a lovely lunch dish if you serve it with a crisp green salad.

Serves 4
10 new potatoes, cut in half
1 onion, chopped into chunks
1 sweet red pepper, chopped finely
4 bacon rashers, chopped
4 eggs
1 tbsp chopped parsley
olive oil and butter, for frying

Preparation
Put the new potatoes in a pan of boiling water. When they are cooked, remove from the pan and slice.

In your large frying pan, heat equal amounts of olive oil and butter, then tip in the onion, red pepper and bacon and cook for 3–4 minutes, or until the bacon starts to looked cooked; make sure you stir the mixture in the pan to prevent burning.

Meanwhile in a large mixing bowl, whisk the eggs till they are light and fluffy.

Add the potatoes to the frying pan and continue stirring the mixture in the pan. When the potatoes start to look golden around the edge, pour the whisked eggs into the pan and add the chopped parsley. Stir the mixture around carefully; otherwise the eggs will just sit on the top. Then turn the heat right down, and cook very gently. After about 2 minutes, slide a pallet knife around the edge of the pan, just to stop it sticking to the edge, then carefully slide the pallet knife underneath the omelette to prevent it sticking to the bottom of the pan. Keep the pan on a low heat until the middle of the omelette is soft and mousselike to the touch. This should take about 7 minutes.

Serve immediately from the pan.

roast peppers
with goat's cheese

These make a perfect accompaniment to some of the lovely salamis and hams you might find while foraging in a local market or deli while on holiday.

Serves 4
2 red peppers
2 yellow peppers
10cm/4in roll of goat's cheese
100g/3½oz pesto
2 large handfuls rocket

Preparation
Preheat the oven to 200°C/400°F/Gas mark 6.
   Top, tail and seed the peppers, then slice into four flat pieces. Slice the goat's cheese into 16 slices.
   Place the peppers in your oven dish, and put 1 teaspoon pesto on each pepper slice, then place a slice of goat's cheese on top. Cover with tin foil and bake in the oven for 25 minutes.
   Serve on a bed of rocket.

3. MAINS

All the mains dishes have been tried and tested many times by my family – and these are our favourites. I have also included a Slow Cooker (pages 82–91) and a Barbecue (pages 92–107) section in this chapter. Both of these cooking methods are fantastic options for caravanning, but of course you can make any of these recipes using your conventional cooker if you prefer.

chicken natasha

If you don't feel like firing up the barbecue, this is a great chicken dish that's quick and simple. It's a personal favourite of mine and I called it Natasha after my little niece, who loves it as much as I do.

Serves 4
4 chicken breasts, skin removed
1 large or 2 small onions, finely chopped
100ml/3½fl oz/scant ½ cup white wine
5 tsp pesto
300ml/10fl oz/1¼ cups double cream
olive oil, for frying

Preparation
Preheat the oven to 220°C/425°F/Gas mark 7.
   Put the chicken breasts in an ovenproof dish, then pour over water to a depth of about 1cm/½in and cover with tin foil. The chicken should take about 25 minutes to cook, but this slightly depends on the thickness.
   Heat the oil in a large frying pan and gently cook the onions. When they are opaque or glassy, add the wine; there will be a fantastic hiss as it hits the pan. Let the wine simmer until reduced to about 1 tablespoon.
   Add the pesto, stirring all the time so that it does not stick to the pan.
   If chicken is not ready, this is fine; just take the sauce off the heat!
   When the chicken is cooked, pour the liquid from the dish into your sauce and stir. Add the double cream and bring to a good simmer. Pour the sauce over the chicken breasts, then serve.

pork chops in a chive sauce

The chive sauce is really easy to make and goes perfectly with pork. You could also use it to accompany the Barbecued Loin of Pork recipe on page 106.

Serves 4

1 onion, sliced
2 celery sticks, sliced
200ml/7fl oz/generous ³/₄ cup white wine or cider
200ml/7fl oz/generous ³/₄ cup stock
   (made from half a stock cube)
225ml/8fl oz/scant 1 cup double cream
2 tbsp chopped chives
4 pork chops
olive oil

Preparation

In a small frying pan, heat some oil and fry the onion and celery until glassy. Pour in the white wine and stock and let the liquid reduce by about half, then add the double cream and finally the chives.

Meanwhile, cook your chops on a skillet pan; they won't take long, depending on the thickness. When the chops are ready, pour the pan juices into your sauce; it will enhance the flavour of the sauce.

Spoon your sauce over the sizzling chops and serve immediately.

spaghetti bolognese

Every one has their own recipe for Spaghetti Bolognese. In recent years, my husband Rowland has developed a good cooking style, but this doesn't extend to Spaghetti Bolognese. One evening, our daughter Ella asked Rowland, 'What's for dinner?' When he told her it was Spaghetti Bolognese, the car fell silent, then she gently asked who was making it – Mum or Dad. On being told it was Mum, Ella was heard to mutter a relieved 'Yes!'

I use beans so that the sauce is light and not as meaty as it can be sometimes. See what you think.

Serves 4
spaghetti for 4
2 onions, chopped
2 celery sticks, chopped
600g/1lb 5oz minced beef
500g/1lb 2oz jar tomato and basil sauce
400g/14oz canned adzuki beans
olive oil, for frying
Parmesan cheese, to serve

Preparation
Put a pan of water on the boil for the spaghetti with a slug of olive oil. When your water is really bubbling, tip in the spaghetti.
    Meanwhile, heat some oil in a frying pan, then cook the onions and celery until glassy. Add the beef, turning it over to make sure it cooks quickly. Once the beef changes colour, add the tomato and basil sauce and simmer for about 10 minutes. Finally, add the beans to heat through.
    Serve immediately, and don't forget the Parmesan!

tagliatelle with prawns and spinach

This is a fantastic recipe for getting kids to eat spinach. Our kids constantly remind me of the terrible day back in 1999 when I made them try spinach soup, but they all love this dish. Try to use young spinach leaves.

Serves 4
200g/7oz spinach
tagliatelle for 4
1 onion, chopped finely
2 celery sticks, chopped finely
3 heaped tsp pesto
300ml/10fl oz/1¼ cups Riesling white wine
300g/10½oz prawns
200ml/7fl oz/generous ¾ cup double cream
olive oil, for frying
Parmesan cheese, to serve

Preparation
Soak the spinach in cold water in the sink.

Cook the pasta in a large pan, remembering to add a generous dollop of olive oil to the water!

Heat a dash of oil in a large frying pan and gently fry the onions and celery till opaque but not brown. Spoon in the pesto and stir once around the pan, then add the wine. Simmer for about 5 minutes, stirring occasionally until the sauce has reduced by about one-third.

Tip into the pan all the spinach, stirring it to make sure it is covered by the liquid. Once the spinach is in the pan, cut it with scissors so that the leaves are a more manageable size. (I know this sounds strange, but it is the best way to cut the spinach without it bruising.) The spinach will wilt almost immediately.

As soon as the spinach has softened, add the prawns and the double cream. Bring it very gently to a simmer, stirring the sauce all the time. When it has simmered for a few minutes, it is ready to serve.

Drain the pasta and serve it straight onto the plates, spooning your delicious sauce on top.

Serve with Parmesan cheese.

seared tuna on a bed of rocket and beetroot

This is a wonderful evening meal – so easy to prepare and it looks fantastic.

I choose small but thick pieces of tuna, so that it stays moist.

Serves 4
60g/2¹/₄oz/generous ²/₃ cup rocket
2 raw beetroot, peeled and grated
50g/1³/₄oz/scant ¹/₄ cup butter
juice of 1 lemon
dash olive oil
4 tuna steaks
4 garlic cloves, peeled and crushed
salt, to taste

Preparation
Prepare your cooking area so that you have room to put the plates out ready.
Put a little bunch of rocket and grated beetroot on top on each plate, so that
when the tuna is cooked you can place it straight on top.

In a skillet pan, heat the butter, lemon juice and a good dash of olive oil.
When it is hot, cook the tuna steaks. After about 3 minutes – the cooking time
will depend on the thickness of the steak – turn the steaks and then add the
garlic to the pan juices.

When ready, place each steak on top of the rocket and beetroot and pour
over some of the pan juice, then season with a pinch of salt.

Serve immediately.

five-minute stir-fry

This dish is truly delicious: the beef literally melts in the mouth. You will have your neighbours craning their necks to find out what you are cooking!

I like to use beef fillet; it's easier to slice thinly. You will need to marinate the beef in advance – the longer you can leave the meat, the better. I do this in the morning and leave it covered in the fridge all day.

Serves 4
600g/1lb 5oz lean beef
teriyaki marinade
edamame beans (soya beans)
toasted sesame oil
nut oil, such as walnut or groundnut
1 sweet red pepper, sliced into matchsticks
4 spring onions, finely chopped
4 garlic cloves, chopped into dice
3cm/1$\frac{1}{4}$in piece of ginger, peeled and grated
100g/3$\frac{1}{2}$oz/1 cup sugar snaps
100g/3$\frac{1}{2}$oz/$\frac{1}{2}$ cup baby sweetcorn, sliced lengthways
400g/14oz pre-cooked egg noodles
350g/12oz/2$\frac{1}{3}$ cups beans sprouts
salt and pepper to taste

Preparation

Cut the beef into thin strips, no more than 1cm/^{1}/$_2$in thick. Put into a bowl and cover with the teriyaki marinade. Leave to marinate in the fridge for at least 30 minutes – and up to all day.

Bring a pan of water to the boil, then add the edamame beans and cook for 4 minutes. Drain in a sieve and refresh under the cold tap; otherwise, they will continue to cook and lose their firmness.

Heat a wok, then pour in 1 tablespoon of each oil, taking care because it does spit. Once the oil is sizzling hot, throw in all the beef, turning constantly, so the strips cook evenly. This will take about 2 minutes, but it slightly depends on the thickness of the beef. Take care not to overcook the beef. Tip the beef from the wok into a sieve over a bowl to catch the juices and leave to stand.

Return the wok to the heat, adding a dash more of each oil to cook the vegetables. First put in the red pepper and the spring onion, followed quickly by the garlic, ginger, sugar snaps and baby sweetcorn, turning all the time. Then add the egg noodles, which will take about 1 minute, still turning all the time. Finally, add the bean sprouts, which warm through really quickly. At this point, pour the meat juice back into the wok, turn it all over for a moment and then add the beef.

Season to taste and serve immediately.

four bean casserole

This is a cosy recipe if the weather is bad and you feel like some comfort food. It is really quick to prepare.

If some of the beans are hard to find, substitute chickpeas or red kidney beans.

Serves 4
1 stock cube (vegetable or beef)
300ml/10fl oz/1^1/$_4$ cups boiling water
2 onions, finely chopped
4 celery sticks, finely chopped
400g/14oz canned butter beans
400g/14oz canned black-eyed beans
400g/14oz canned adzuki beans
400g/14oz canned cannellini beans
1 tbsp tomato purée
100ml/3^1/$_2$fl oz/scant ^{1}/$_2$ cup double cream
2 pinches dried thyme
2 pinches dried tarragon
salt and pepper, to taste
olive oil

Preparation
Dissolve the stock cube in the boiling water.
   Put a dash of olive oil in a large pan and heat on the hob. When sizzling, add the onions and celery and cook for about 5 minutes, then add all the beans with the stock and the tomato purée. Bring to a simmer and keep simmering for a further 10 minutes. Add the double cream and dried herbs, then season with salt and pepper.
   Serve immediately.

pesto pasta with pea and ham

This is a perfect first-night dish. You should be able to get all the ingredients, and it's a nice, quick, easy meal if you have been map reading or, worse still, putting up the awning!

Serves 4
500g/1lb 2oz dried fusilli pasta
200g/7oz/2 cups peas (fresh or frozen)
1 onion, chopped
300ml/10fl oz/1$^{1}/_{4}$ cups white wine
6 ham slices, cut into dice
4 tbsp pesto
220ml/7$^{1}/_{2}$fl oz/generous 3 cups double cream
olive oil
Parmesan cheese, to serve

Preparation
Put a large pan of water of the boil with a dash of olive oil, and when it comes to the boil add the pasta.

Meanwhile, put of a little pan of water and cook the peas; fresh peas will take a little longer than frozen. When the peas are cooked, strain and set to one side.

Gently cook the onion in a pan till glassy, then pour in the wine and cook for about 5 minutes to let the wine reduce by about one-third. Add the ham and pesto, turning it over in the pan, then add the peas and the cream and bring to a gentle simmer; do not let it boil.

When the pasta is cooked, drain the pasta and serve immediately, spooning the sauce over each potion of pasta.

Serve with plenty of Parmesan and a salad.

cod in parsley sauce

If you've been eating out and had lots of rich food, this cleansing and homely dish is the perfect solution. It is heavenly served with minted new potatoes.

You can also make this recipe with coley. It has a more dense flesh than cod, and so makes for a heartier meal.

Serves 4
850g/1lb 14oz cod fillets
sukiyaki sauce, optional
300ml/10fl oz/1¼ cups water
1 onion, chopped
2 celery sticks, chopped
200ml/7fl oz/generous ¾ cup white wine
220ml/7½fl oz/generous 3 cups double cream
3 tbsp chopped parsley, chopped

Preparation
Preheat the oven to 200°C/400°F/Gas mark 6.
  Put the fish in an ovenproof dish and sprinkle over a little sukiyaki sauce and the water. Cover with tin foil and bake in the oven for 20 minutes.
  Meanwhile, in a frying pan, sauté the onion and celery till glassy, then add the white wine and simmer for 5 minutes. Set aside.
  When the fish is cooked, bring it out of the oven and pour the liquid from the oven dish into the onion, celery and wine in the frying pan, making sure you leave a small amount in the dish so that the fish doesn't dry out. Cover the fish dish with the foil and it will retain its heat. Simmer the liquid for 3–4 minutes, or until it has reduced by one-third. Add the double cream and parsley, then gently bring to a simmer.
  Serve the fish straight onto the plates and spoon over a generous amount of sauce.

one-pan sausage cider

This is a recipe that I made up years ago and it has passed the test of time. It is a great one if you are feeding a lot of hungry people because it is a hearty dish that is very simple to prepare.

Serves 4
4 tomatoes
2 leeks
2 onions
1 sweet red pepper
8 pork sausages
4 garlic cloves, peeled and sliced into quarters
400ml/14fl oz/scant 1¾ cups cider
400g/14oz canned butter beans
handful parsley, finely chopped
olive oil, for frying

Preparation
Slice the tomatoes from top to bottom into 8–10 segments. Slice the leeks, onions and sweet red pepper; this dish is a hearty one, so the vegetables can be quite chunky.

In a large frying pan, start to fry the sausages. When they are nicely brown all over – after about 15 minutes – tip in the onions, shortly followed by the red pepper. Keep turning the vegetable and the sausages gently so that nothing burns. When the onions have softened – after 4–5 minutes – add the leeks, tomatoes and garlic. When the tomatoes have started to disintegrate, add the cider and butter beans and simmer until the liquid has reduced by one-third. Take off the heat and sprinkle with a generous amount of parsley.

Serve with some crusty bread.

swordfish with basil and lime

This is a real favourite with the kids and so easy. I've used swordfish here, but the recipe works just as well with tuna or coley.

Serves 4
4 swordfish steaks
juice of 2 limes
10 basil leaves, finely chopped
olive oil and butter, for frying

Preparation
In a skillet pan, heat equal amounts of oil and butter. When sizzling, place the fish on the skillet. Just before turning the fish, drizzle over half the lime juice and then turn and cook the other side. When that side is cooked, drizzle over the remaining lime juice, and turn one more time to seal the juice. The cooking time depends on the thickness of the steak, but it won't take long.

Serve immediately, pouring the pan juices over the swordfish and sprinkling with basil.

Delicious with minty, buttery new potatoes.

rivron tandoori chicken

This one will turn your caravan neighbours green with envy. There is something about the smell of Indian food …

Serves 4
3 heaped tsp tandoori curry powder
300g/10^1/$_2$oz/scant 1^1/$_2$ cups natural yogurt
4 chicken breasts
olive oil, for frying

Preparation
Mix the curry powder and the yogurt in a large Tupperware box (which will hold all the chicken breasts), then add the chicken breasts, making sure they are all covered with the curried yogurt. Leave in the fridge, preferably overnight; if not, do this first thing in the morning, ready for the evening meal.
    In a skillet pan, fry the marinated chicken breast in a small amount of olive oil, until the chicken is cooked through. Serve with rice and salad.

pumpkin curry

If pumpkin is not in season, butternut squash makes a delicious substitute.

Serves 4

1 pumpkin – you need a total of 1kg/2lb 4oz pumpkin flesh
1 onion, chopped
1 tsp cumin
1 tsp turmeric
1 tsp ground coriander
1 large pinch cayenne pepper
3 red chillies, deseeded and finely chopped
600ml/1 pint/2½ cups chicken or vegetable stock, made from a stock cube
200ml/7fl oz/generous ¾ cup coconut milk
olive oil and butter, for cooking

Preparation

Peel and slice the pumpkin into chunks.

In a large saucepan, melt the butter and the olive oil. When it is sizzling, add the onion and cook for a few moments, then add the cumin, turmeric, ground coriander, cayenne and red chilli. Tip in the pumpkin chunks and turn them around in the pan, making sure they are all covered in the lovely buttery oil. Pour in the stock and simmer for about 15 minutes; take care not to overcook the pumpkin because you want it to keep its shape.

When the pumpkin is cooked, drain the liquid into another pan, and put the spicy pumpkin to one side. Bring the liquid to the boil and simmer to reduce and thicken, as this will make a lovely spicy sauce. Pour the sauce back over the spicy pumpkin and add the coconut milk. Bring to a gentle simmer.

Serve immediately with rice or leave to cool, then reheat and and serve later.

sesame salmon with edamame beans

This is a dish that will suit all palates and can be thrown together very quickly. All the ingredients can be found in high street supermarkets. In my local supermarket, edamame beans go by the name of soya beans. They come in little packets of 200g/7oz and have been precooked.

Serves 4
1 egg
2 tbsp plain flour
2 tbsp sesame seeds
4 salmon fillets
100g/3¹/₂oz/2 cups sliced button mushrooms
400g/14oz edamame beans (soya beans)
5 garlic cloves, peeled and sliced with the
   inner root removed
2cm/³/₄in piece of ginger, peeled and sliced into thin strips
sukiyaki sauce
sesame oil or olive oil and butter, for frying

Preparation
Beat the egg and pour it into a large dish. Sieve the flour and tip into a second large dish, then add the sesame seeds and shake the dish so the flour and seeds are all mixed in.

Put the salmon in the flour mixture and make sure the fillets have a covering of flour. Place them in the egg dish, and coat with the beaten egg, and then put back in the flour dish for a seconding coating. Put the salmon on a plate and cover until ready to fry. This can be done earlier in the day and left in the fridge if you wish.

Heat a wok on the hob with a little olive oil, then throw in the mushroom and cook, turning all the time to prevent burning. Add the beans, garlic, ginger and a good shake of sukiyaki sauce and cook for a further 2 minutes. Put to one side.

Heat a frying pan with sesame oil, if you have it, or olive oil and a little butter. When there are tiny bubbles, turn the heat right down. Carefully place the salmon in the pan and cook, turning the fish after about 4 minutes. Cook for another 4 minutes. (This timing may vary, depending on the thickness of the salmon). Check the salmon is done by cutting into one at the thickest point. When the fish is cooked, take the pan off the heat.

Then return the wok to the hob and bring up the beans to a steaming temperature, turning all the time for 1 minute.

Serve the salmon with the beans on one side.

rolled loin of lamb

I used to cook this only at home, but when I came across a beautiful cut of lamb in a little French boucherie I couldn't resist trying it in the caravan and found it works just as well. If you don't want to remove the fat from the loin yourself, you can ask your butcher to do this; or you may even come across pre-prepared loins in the supermarket.

Serves 4
1 loin of lamb with 4 bones
4 garlic bulbs, peeled and sliced
4 rosemary sprigs, chopped finely
string

Preparation
Preheat the oven to 200°C/400°F/Gas mark 6.

Carefully remove the layer of fat from the meat, so that it comes away in one piece; I find a boning knife is ideal for this. You will wrap the meat back up in the fat, so you need to make sure it comes away in one rectangular piece. Pull the fat from the flesh, and with the tip of the knife gently score where the meat meets the fat. Put the fat to one side.

Now you have to remove the bone. This cut is basically two tubes of meat, a larger one and a smaller one on each side of the bone. Gently keeping the tip of the knife on the bone, slowly cut the flesh away. This sounds harder than it is: if you make sure your knife scrapes the bone, you won't have a problem. You will end up with two beautiful tubes of loin of lamb.

Lay the fat out flat between two pieces of clingfilm, then flatten by bashing it with a rolling pin. This will break up any hard lumps of fat. Remove the top layer of clingfilm and place your two tubes of meat on the fat, putting the garlic and rosemary evenly all over the meat. Then roll the meat inside the fat and tie it securely with string. I use about five pieces of string, just to be on the safe side. I start by tying it together from the middle and work outwards. It should end up looking like a little Swiss roll, trussed up in string.

Cook the lamb in the oven for about 25 minutes. The timing of this will vary slightly, depending on the size and how well you like your lamb cooked. Check after 25 minutes by cutting into in the middle and taking a look.

When you take it out of the oven, leave it to rest for at least 5 minutes before you carve it. Cover it in a clean tea towel and it will keep warm.

mediterranean chicken

This recipe is fantastic if you are missing your Sunday Roast. The added bonus is that on holiday you're likely to find far tastier tomatoes and olives than you might get in your supermarket at home.

Serves 4
4 chicken supremes
250g/9oz/1¼ cups cherry tomatoes, sliced in half
150g/5½oz/scant 1 cup black olives, pitted
5 garlic cloves, crushed
handful herbes de Provence
handful parsley, finely chopped
olive oil
salt and pepper, to taste

Preparation
Preheat the oven to 200°C/400°F/Gas mark 6.
   Place the chicken supremes in your large oven dish, skin side up, and drizzle with olive oil. Throw over the cherry tomatoes and the olives, then sprinkle over the crushed garlic and herbs. Season with salt and pepper and bake in the oven for 40 minutes.
   To serve, sprinkle over the parsley and serve with rice, bread or even pommes frites from the camp café!

... SLOW COOKER

I really recommend buying a slow cooker. Some have timers, others switch themselves off after 2 hours. Either way, you can prepare your evening meal in the morning, stick it in the cooker and go off and enjoy your day without having to worry about getting back to prepare food, or worse, leaving the caravan with the cooker on!

slow lamb casserole

This dish is fantastic for a caravan holiday. You can make it in the morning, go out for the day and come back to a delicious meal waiting for you.

For this, I like to use the neck of lamb, but leg is just as good.

Serves 4
750g/1lb 10oz lamb, cut into cubes
2 onions, chopped
2 celery sticks, chopped
300ml/10fl oz/1$\frac{1}{2}$ cups red wine
500g/1lb 2oz jar of tomato and basil sauce
canned chickpeas
dash of double cream
olive oil, for frying

Preparation
Turn on the slow cooker to Medium.

Heat a dash of olive oil in large frying pan, then sear the lamb. Sear only small amounts at a time, as you want to keep the pan as hot has possible – the quicker the lamb is seared, the more tender it will be. Place the lamb in the slow cooker.

Pan-fry the onions for a few moments, then add the celery and tip that into the slow cooker. Deglaze the pan with the wine – to clean up all the lovely bits of meat and vegetables left in the pan – by simmering the wine for at least 2 minutes, then tip into the casserole.

Pour the tomato and basil sauce into the slow cooker and add the chickpeas. Cook for 2 hours, then leave the casserole on warm for as long as you can – all day if you like. (If you are making this in a conventional oven, cook for 2 hours at 150°C/300°F/Gas mark 2.)
Just before you serve, add a dash of double cream.

Serve with rice or mash.

soup bowl chicken

The reason I call this Soup Bowl Chicken is that I serve this in a bowl and we eat it with spoons and chunky bread. It's the most wonderful thing, especially if you want something cosy and warming. It's a great dish if the weather has forced you inside and you're all eating round the table in the caravan; there's hardly any washing up and you're not wrestling with large plates in a small space.

Serves 4
4 chicken breasts, cut into bite-size pieces
4 bacon rashers, finely chopped
2 onions, sliced
2 sticks of celery, sliced
300ml/10fl oz/1½ cups Alsace white wine
500ml/18fl oz/generous 2 cups chicken stock (made from a stock cube)
3 leeks, sliced
400g/14oz canned butter beans
400g/14oz canned chickpeas
400g/14oz canned sweetcorn
dash of double cream
olive oil, for pan-frying

Preparation
Turn on the slow cooker to Medium.

Heat some olive oil in a pan and fry the chicken, just to seal it, then tip into the slow cooker. Cook the bacon bits and again tip into the cooker, then finally fry the onions and celery and add to the cooker. Pour the wine into the frying-pan and simmer thoroughly for 2–3 minutes, then pour into the cooker.

Add the chicken stock, then the leeks, butter beans, chickpeas and sweetcorn (including the water from the cans as well). Put the lid on the slow cooker and go off and enjoy your day ... (If you are making this on the hob, place a lid on the pan and gently simmer for 30 minutes.)

... When you return, all you have to do is add the double cream and serve with bread.

lettuce soup

This soup takes me back to my own childhood. My Mum used to make it on summer days and I have always associated this soup with long happy summer days in the garden. It was this soup that made me realise I was really interested in food.

Serves 4
3 large or 5 small spring onions, chopped
100ml/3$^{1}/_{2}$fl oz/scant $^{1}/_{2}$ cup white wine
1 salad lettuce, sliced
1 litre/1$^{3}/_{4}$ pints/4 cups chicken stock, made from 2 stock cubes
200ml/7fl oz/generous $^{3}/_{4}$ cup double cream
1 tablespoon coriander, chopped
butter, for frying

Preparation
Turn on the slow cooker to High.

Sauté the spring onions in a little knob of butter for 2 minutes, then add the wine and lettuce and cook for a further 3 minutes. Tip into the slow cooker and add the stock, then leave to slow cook for about 30 minutes. (If you are making this on the hob, simmer gently for 20 minutes. Ensure that the soup does not come to the boil at any point.) Take the casserole dish out of the slow cooker and blend the soup with a hand blender. Add the double cream, then sprinkle over the coriander.

Serve immediately or leave to cool and then reheat to serve later.

thai green curry

Serves 4

4 chicken breasts, skinned and
    boned, then cut into cubes
150g/5$^{1}/_{2}$oz chestnut mushrooms,
    cut in half
100ml/3$^{1}/_{2}$fl oz/scant $^{1}/_{2}$ cup water
1 stock cube
1 tablespoon nam pla sauce (Thai
    fish sauce)
canned coconut milk
8 lime leaves
1 tablespoon coriander leaves,
    chopped
1 tablespoon sweet basil leaves,
    chopped
olive oil and nut oil, for frying

Green Curry Paste

4 lemongrass stalks
6 green chillies, deseeded and
    chopped
3 garlic cloves, chopped
5cm/2in piece of ginger, chopped
2 shallots, chopped
4 tablespoons chopped coriander
1 tsp cumin
1 tsp coriander
juice of $^{1}/_{2}$ lime
1 tablespoon nam pla (Thai fish
    sauce)

Curries are not traditionally associated with caravans, for several reasons: they can be labour-intensive and create lots of washing-up, and in the confines of a caravan the aroma can outstay its welcome. There are no such worries with this one: I make it in the slow cooker and there is very little washing up. It's simple to prepare, and the result is both authentic and delicious.

You can buy green curry paste ready made, but if you have the time and the inclination it's a lot more rewarding to make your own and is surprisingly quick and easy.

Preparation

Make the curry paste first. Slice the lemongrass stalks, using only the softer insides of the lemongrass; the outer leaves can be very tough. Put all the paste ingredients in a large jam jar and use your handheld blender to blend away; the smell is amazing. You won't get the paste really smooth – don't worry. Put to one side until you are ready to use.
    Turn on the slow cooker to High. Heat a little olive oil and nut oil in a pan, then seal the chicken in batches, just till it changes colour on the outside. Tip the chicken into the slow cooker. Fry the mushrooms and when they have gone a golden colour tip them into the slow cooker. Deglaze the pan with the water and stock cube and nam pla sauce, letting the stock cube disintegrate by mixing it around in the pan, then add to the slow cooker. Finally add the coconut milk, lime leaves and fresh herbs to the cooker, then pop the lid on and leave for 1 hour. (If you are making this on the hob, place a lid on the pan and gently simmer for 30 minutes.)
    Serve with rice.

butternut squash soup

This is a lovely warming soup with a rich sweet flavour, and is very simple and easy to prepare. I recommend this soup for children who don't like vegetables; they will like this one!

Serves 4
2 butternut squash or 1 large squash – you need 500g/1lb 2oz
    squash once it has been peeled
2 tablespoons butter
2 onions, sliced
1 celery stick, sliced
800ml/1¹/₃ pints/scant 3¹/₄ cups stock, made from a stock cube
large pinch nutmeg
dash olive oil

Preparation
Peel and cut the squash into small cubes. Turn on the slow cooker to High.

In your pan, melt the butter and oil. When sizzling, add the onion and celery, turning around in the pan for about 2 minutes, then add the squash. Keep turning until all the squash is covered in the butter, which should take no more than 1 minute. Tip the contents of the pan into the slow cooker, and then pour the stock into the pan to clean up all the juices in the pan. Next, pour these juices into the slow cooker. Add the nutmeg, then put the lid on the slow cooker and leave for 1 hour. (If you are making this on the hob, place a lid on the pan and gently simmer for 30 minutes.)

Turn off the slow cooker and use a handheld blender to blend the soup in the slow cooker itself.

Serve immediately, or leave to cool and reheat later.

whole chicken in cider

This is a wonderful dish, and it is so exciting that you can cook a whole chicken without using half a gas canister. This meal is absolutely delicious and, because it is cooked in the slow cooker, takes very little effort.

Serves 4
1 whole chicken
1 large or 2 small onions, chopped into large chunks
2 leeks, sliced
2 garlic cloves, sliced
500ml/18fl oz/generous 2 cups cider
500ml/18fl oz/generous 2 cups chicken stock, made from a stock cube
1 pinch saffron
2 pinches tarragon
100ml/3^1/2fl oz/scant ^{1}/2 cup double cream
olive oil

Preparation
Turn on the slow cooker to High. Wipe the chicken.

In a large frying pan, heat the oil and cook the onions for 2 minutes. Add the leeks and garlic, turning them continuously in the pan, and cook for a further 2 minutes. Tip them into the slow cooker. Pour the cider into the frying pan and heat to deglaze the pan. When the cider is bubbling, pour it into the slow cooker. Put the whole chicken into the slow cooker, breast side down, then pour in the stock, making sure the chicken is covered, and sprinkle over the saffron and tarragon. Put the lid on and leave it to cook for at least 2 hours. About 30 minutes before you want to serve, turn the chicken, breast side up.

(If you make this in a conventional oven, ensure you use a dish small enough to hold the chicken snugly, or it will fall apart during cooking. Cook in a conventional oven for 2 hours at 150°C/300°F/Gas mark 2.)

Just before serving, pour in the double cream.

I serve this dish with a big bowl of peas and French bread.

... LIGHTING A BARBIE

There is a certain time of day, when you're back from the beach and all cleaned up, and you're aware that around the campsite all the barbecues are being fired up and all manner of delicious things are being cooked. You don't need to mess around too much with meat and fish cooked on the barbecue but I've provided some great marinades and side dishes. Rowland always, takes control of the tongs while I prepare the accompaniments. One year Rowland was so proud of his skills, we had to wait while he photographed every piece of meat!

My Top 3 BBQ tips

* Always clean your barbie after every use
* Once you've cleaned and dried the grill, oil it, to prevent anything sticking
* Be patient! Don't start cooking until your coals have turned grey

tzatziki

If you are barbecuing lamb, it is lovely to have tzatziki with it. It is so easy to make and the homemade version is so much tastier.

300ml/10fl oz/1¼ cups Greek yogurt
one-third of a cucumber
8 mint leaves

Preparation
Cut the cucumber into very small cubes. Put the mint leaves into a jam jar and cut with scissors; doing this in a jar stops the mint leaves getting everywhere.
   Combine all the ingredients and serve as an accompaniment to lamb.

garlic mayonnaise

I always keep a jam jar of garlic mayonnaise in the fridge. All I do is crush 6 garlic cloves into a jam jar and then spoon in Hellman's and stir. It is just so useful.

moroccan chickpea side dish

This is a perfect side dish for barbecued lamb and is very simple to prepare. I made up this recipe for Rowland when he took part in *Celebrity Britain's Best Dish* and the judges loved it.

Serves 4
1 onion, finely chopped
1 celery stick, finely chopped
3 garlic cloves, crushed
150g/5 oz/scant 1 cup cherry tomatoes, cut into quarters
2–3 small red chillies, deseeded and finely chopped
250ml/8fl oz/1 cup white wine
300ml/10fl oz/1¼ cups stock
½ tsp cumin
¼ tsp paprika
400g/14oz canned chickpeas
salt and pepper, for seasoning
olive oil, for frying

Preparation
Pan-fry the onions, then add the celery, garlic and tomatoes in that order. Finally, add the chillies, and cook for 2–3 minutes, turning the mixture constantly in the pan to avoid burning. Add the white wine and stock, then simmer for 5 minutes. Add the cumin and paprika, then add the chickpeas and cook for a further 5 minutes. Season with salt and pepper to taste.

buttery asparagus

There is nothing more delicious than asparagus with dripping butter.

Serves 4
200g/7oz asparagus
butter
parsley, finely chopped

Preparation
Bend each stem of the asparagus; where it snaps is the exact point that it will become tough to eat. So just break off these tough, thick ends.

Bring a pan of water to the boil and put the asparagus in, then simmer for 5 minutes. They need to be firm yet tender.

Serve with a generous amount of butter and finely chopped parsley.

courgettes with garlic and parsley

This is almost a meal in itself; it has a lovely fresh taste and is the perfect dish to accompany barbecued lamb.

Serves 4
6 courgettes
1 tbsp butter
slug olive oil
juice of $1/2$ lemon
4 garlic cloves, crushed
1 tbsp pine nuts
1 tbsp parsley, chopped
salt

Preparation
Top and tail the courgettes and slice lengthways into quarters.

In a large frying pan, melt the butter gently, then add the olive oil and lemon juice and place the courgettes in the pan. Cook gently for 2–3 minutes, then turn the courgettes over and add the garlic. Cook for 1 minute, then add the pine nuts, taking care not to burn them. When both flesh sides of the courgettes looks nicely golden brown, tip onto a serving dish.

Sprinkle with parsley and salt. Serve immediately.

baby vegetables

This is an easy way to serve exciting vegetables that the children will love. I often do these at the caravan because it is a really quick way of doing vegetables and they look absolutely lovely.

Serves 4
200g/7oz baby courgettes
200g/7oz baby sweetcorn
parsley, finely chopped
1 tbsp butter
1 tbsp olive oil

Preparation
Top and tail the courgettes and slice them lengthways down the middle. Slicing them before cooking gets rid of the slightly bitter taste.

In a wok or large pan, melt the butter and olive oil, then throw in the vegetables and turn around the wok for about 3 minutes, till the courgettes just start to go golden at the edges.

Sprinkle with parsley and serve immediately.

ratatouille

I always (and I mean always!) make this if we are having a barbecue. Barbecued meat needs something juicy as an accompaniment and this really does the job.

Serves 4
2 onions
5 tomatoes
2 courgettes, sliced
3 garlic cloves, peeled and sliced
200ml/7fl oz/generous ¾ cup white wine
200ml/7fl oz/generous ¾ cup stock
    (made from ½ stock cube)
olive oil, for frying

Preparation
Chop the onion into chunks, and slice each tomato into about 8 pieces.

In a large frying pan, fry the onions for a few minutes, then add the tomatoes and courgettes, turning them around in the pan. When the tomatoes soften, add the wine and stock, then reduce the liquid to one-third.

Serve immediately.

corn on the cob

This all-time favourite gets made again and again on holiday.

Serves 4
4 corn on the cob
100g/3½oz/⅞ stick salted butter, softened
1 dessertspoon parsley, finely chopped
1 dessertspoon coriander, finely chopped

Preparation
Cut the corn cobs in half to make eight smaller chunks.
Cook the cobs in boiling water for 10 minutes. Meanwhile,
mix the herbs with the soft butter. When the corn is ready,
cut them in half, as they are easier to eat when they
are smaller.
   Serve with a few knobs of herb butter on top.

pasta salad for a barbecue

When we have a barbecue, we always make this dish: it can
be served hot, warm or cold. The children tend to eat a nice
big portion while they are waiting for their food to cook,
Rowland and I have it as a little side dish with our
barbecued meat, but either way I find it a very useful and
simple dish.

Serves 4
pasta for four (shells or fusilli)
1 large or 2 small onions, finely chopped
1 sweet red pepper, deseeded and chopped
400g/14oz canned sweetcorn
½ tsp cumin

Preparation
Put the water on the boil with a slug of olive oil.
   When the water is at a furious boil, put in the pasta and
cook according to the packet instructions.
   Meanwhile, in a frying pan gently sauté the onion for a
few minutes. Add the sweet red pepper and cook for an
additional 1 minute, then add the sweetcorn and the cumin.
Cook for a further 2 minutes, turning the mixture around in
the pan to prevent burning.
   When the pasta is cooked, drain it and combine with the
onion and pepper mixture, then serve.

marinated chilli chicken

We barbecue the chicken, but you could just as easily pan-fry it on a skillet pan on the hob. This recipe does have a kick to it, so I sometimes prepare two separate marinades – one with chilli and one without for the children. If so, I always cook the chilli-free chicken first.

Serves 4
4 chicken breasts, skinned and boned
1 green chilli, deseeded and sliced
1 tsp chilli flakes
2 garlic cloves, peeled
1 pinch saffron
20 mint leaves
2 tbsp olive oil
1 tbsp clear honey

Preparation

There is very little chopping in this marinade because you just blend together all the ingredients. Slice the chicken into strips; one breast should slice into three or four strips. Put the strips in a dish.

Put all the remaining ingredients into a jam jar, then use a hand blender to mix them all together. Pour the marinade over the chicken and leave for at least 1 hour.

Now you are ready to cook your chicken. Whether you are cooking this in a skillet pan or on the barbecue, you must remember to turn the chicken every 2 or 3 minutes to prevent it blackening on the outside. The cooking time will depend to some extent on the thickness of your strips, but should be about 15 minutes in total.

salmon in parcels

When I was at cookery school, we used parchment paper for this recipe, which was quite fiddly. Now I use foil, which is so much simpler. This is a lovely dish: you cook the portion of vegetables in the parcel with the fish.

Serves 4
2 leeks
2 carrots
4 salmon fillets
100g/3^1/$_2$oz/^{7}/$_8$ stick butter
dried thyme
dried oregano
fresh parsley, finely chopped

Preparation
Preheat the oven to 200°C/400°F/Gas mark 6.

Remove the outer skin of the leeks and peel the carrots, then slice both vegetables into matchsticks.

Place one salmon fillet on a square of foil and put some matchsticks of leeks and carrots on top of the fish. Then put two knobs of butter and a pinch each of thyme and oregano and a sprinkle of parsley.

Wrap up the parcel like a pasty, and then bake in the oven for 15 minutes.

To serve, open up each parcel and plate the salmon, then pour over the buttery juices. This is great with minty new potatoes.

chicken breast in foil

This is never off the barbecue when we're caravanning. It is so easy, and the foil stops the chicken from getting dry. Just cook as many chicken breasts as you need for the number of people.

chicken breasts
butter
garlic, peeled and sliced
parsley, finely chopped

Preparation
Place each chicken breast on a square of aluminium foil. Slice open the chicken breast and put a knob of butter, some slices of garlic and 1 teaspoon parsley in the middle. Close the breast back together and wrap securely in the foil. Place each parcel on the barbecue, turning every 6–7 minutes. This takes about 25 minutes; I am always surprised by how long chicken takes.

To serve, open up each foil parcel and pour all the lovely buttery juice over the chicken.

garlic linguine with sausages

This dish is wonderful for a hungry family, and it's a great one if you have been out all day. You can quickly fire up the barbecue, get the sausages on – and away you go. It's a bit of a dash at the end, but it is well worth it.

Serves 4
8 pork sausages
500g/1lb 2oz linguine
4 garlic cloves, crushed
2 tbsp parsley, finely chopped
olive oil

Preparation
Prepare the barbecue, then put the sausages on to cook.

Meanwhile, put on a large pan of water to boil, adding a dash of olive oil to the water. Once your sausages are cooked, tip your linguine into the boiling water.

Slice the cooked sausages into pieces about 2cm/¾in thick.

Pour 3–4 tablespoons olive oil into a large baking tray, then put on the hob to heat it up. (Be careful; the tray heats up very quickly.) Put the sausage slices and garlic in the baking tray and stir it all around until the sausages are covered in the lovely garlic oil. Turn off the gas under the baking tray.

If the pasta is ready before this is complete, just turn off the heat and leave the pasta sitting in the water; it will be fine.

Strain the pasta and tip it all into the baking tray, turning it over so that the linguine is covered in garlic and sausage.

Throw over the parsley and serve.

marinated lamb chops

Lamb is so delicious marinated, and this is such an easy marinade. I make up the marinade in the morning and put the chops in, cover the dish with clingfilm and leave it for the day. Our fridge is always full to bursting, so I leave the marinating chops in the turned-off oven because I figure it is probably the coolest place in the caravan!

Serves 4
lamb chops for 4

Marinade
juice of 1 lemon
6 garlic cloves, crushed
$1/2$ tsp dried thyme
$1/2$ tsp dried oregano
250ml/8fl oz/1 cup olive oil

Preparation
Put the marinade ingredients into a large dish and stir with a wooden spoon. Put the chops in the marinade, and turn at least once during the day. They only need about 1 hour to marinate, but you get a better flavour the longer you leave them.

Slap the chops on the barbecue (or pan-fry them in a skillet pan). The size of the chops and how you like them cooked will determine cooking time, but a medium lamb chop cooked slightly pink in the middle should take about 5 minutes on each side.

barbecued loin of pork

This is a great cut of meat for barbecuing and perfect for a large number of people, if you cook two pieces of meat at the same time. A small loin of pork will serve 4 and a large loin 6. Remember to keep an eye on the meat during cooking, as it needs turning and painting with syrup every 10 minutes.

pork loin
maple syrup

Preparation
Prepare the barbecue, and wash and dry the meat.

First remove the fat from the loin of pork; this is very simple to do, especially if you have a good boning knife. Separate it a little at a time, edging the tip of the knife between the fat and the flesh. Then remove the bone – just keep the tip of the knife firmly against the bone and gently cut the flesh away. You can ask your butcher to do this, or may even find prepared loins in the supermarket, if you don't feel confident about removing the fat and bone yourself.

When the coals are ready, push them all to one side – you don't want to cook the meat directly over the coals or it will burn. Place some foil underneath the grill to collect the drips and to prevent the barbecue from becoming sticky.

Paint one side of your meat with maple syrup and put the non-syrup side on the grill, away from the coals; put the lid on the barbecue. Turn the meat every 10 minutes and paint the top side each time, then replace the lid. The meat will take 40 minutes to cook.

Slice and serve. This is delicious served with the Chive Sauce recipe on page 61.

4. SUNDOWNERS

It is lovely having guests over on a warm evening to swap caravanning adventures or disasters. Everyone has a tale to tell. Here are a few quick nibbles you can make easily and they're so much nicer than a big bag of crisps.

I have also included a section targeted at teenage tummies. Nobody wants to clock watch on holiday and kids frequently return to the caravan 'starving' at all hours of the day and night. These recipes are great standbys – quick to prepare and sure to please a young crowd.

olives in garlic, chilli and parsley

This is a great little marinade that livens up black olives.

160g/5³/4oz/scant 1 cup pitted black olives
200ml/7fl oz/generous ³/4 cup olive oil
3 garlic cloves, finely chopped
1 red chilli, deseeded and finely chopped
1 tbsp finely chopped parsley

Preparation
Drain the olives and put them in a little serving dish. Pour over the olive oil, then add the garlic, chilli and parsley. As with any marinade, these taste better if they are left for a few hours.

spicy nuts

This is a lovely little nibble if fellow caravaners drop by for a drink. Just be prepared for the smoke alarm to go off ... Use a nut oil if you have it; if not, olive oil is fine.

1 tbsp oil
4 dessertspoons caster sugar
2 pinches cumin
3 large pinches chilli flakes
200g/7oz unsalted mixed nuts

Preparation

Use a pastry brush to paint oil around the inside of a wok.

Put the sugar, cumin and chilli flakes into the wok and heat. When your see the sugar start to change colour, add the nuts and turn all the time. This does create smoke, but the process is very quick. Once the sugar turns golden brown, take off the heat immediately. Turn out into a dish, and wait – the nuts will be tongue-burningly hot. You might need to break them up a little, as they sometimes stick together in big chunks.

After 5 minutes, serve.

grilled halloumi

This is one of my favourite little side dishes. It reminds me of beautiful warm evenings.

Serves 4
250g/9oz halloumi
handful parsley, finely chopped
olive oil, for the pan

Preparation
Simply slice the halloumi cheese like a little loaf of bread, each slice being about 5mm/¹/₄in thick.

Pour a very small amount of olive oil into a skillet pan and heat, then fry the halloumi until golden, then turn over and fry the other side.

Sprinkle with parsley and serve.

pan-fried artichoke hearts

These make a lovely dish and are very versatile. You can serve them with barbecued food or with salads.

I never mind using one half of a lemon because I always make good use of the other half. Left in the fridge uncovered for 2–3 days, it keeps the fridge smelling nice and fresh.

Serves 4
280g/10oz canned or jar artichoke hearts
2 tbsp butter
dash olive oil
3 garlic cloves, crushed
juice of $\frac{1}{2}$ lemon
pinch tarragon
1 tsp finely chopped parsley
salt and pepper to taste

Preparation
Drain the artichoke hearts and slice them in half.
    Heat the butter and oil in a frying pan, and when sizzling add the garlic and lemon. Place the artichoke hearts carefully in the pan and sprinkle with the tarragon and parsley. Turn them carefully after 2 minutes and cook for a further 1 minute. Place on a serving dish and pour over the pan juices, then season with salt and pepper.
    Serve immediately.

sugar fried prawns

I make these for the children when Rowland is barbecuing. The children first had something like this at a restaurant and loved them, so I worked out a simplified version. Here it is!

Serves 4
150g/5¹/₂oz king prawns
4 spring onions, finely chopped
150g/5¹/₂oz/1 cup plain flour, sifted
1 tbsp sesame seeds
1 egg
100g/3¹/₂oz/¹/₂ cup granulated sugar
olive oil, for frying
barbecue sticks

Preparation
Cut the barbecues sticks to fit inside the frying pan.
   Peel the prawns if necessary. Feed the prawns onto the sticks, skewering through the top and tail of the prawn (to make the shape of a capital C).
   Put the spring onions into a flat dish with the flour, then add the sesame seeds and mix well. In a second flat dish, crack the egg and whisk in the sugar.
   Dip the skewered prawns in the flour, then dip into the egg batter and then back into the flour. Pan-fry the prawns in olive oil for 2 minutes each side.
   Serve immediately.

whitebait

If you can get fresh whitebait, all the better, but frozen is fine.

Serves 4
450g/16oz fresh or frozen whitebait
75g/2^3/4oz/^{1}/2 cup plain flour seasoned with salt and pepper
300ml/10fl oz/1^1/4 cups olive oil

Preparation
If frozen, allow the whitebait to defrost in the bag it comes in. Put paper towels on the side next to the hob, ready to take the whitebait.

Sift the plain flour into a large dish.

Put the whitebait into the dish of flour and shake the dish until all the fish are covered with flour. Pour the oil into a wok and heat until sizzling. Drop in the first handful of fish; make sure the oil covers the fish and cook for 3 minutes, or until they look crispy. Tip out onto the paper towels, then drop in the next handful and repeat. You may need to top up the oil, so make sure you bring the oil up to the right temperature before dropping in the next handful. One bag usually takes me four goes. The fish retain the temperature well.

Serve immediately with Garlic Mayonnaise (see page 94).

pink lemonade

This is a very refreshing drink on a hot sunny day. There is something about making your own lemonade that gives you such a great feeling. There is nothing better than knowing exactly what has gone into a fizzy drink.

If you want a regular lemonade version, replace the grapefruit with 5 lemons.

200g/7oz/1 cup caster sugar
200ml/7fl oz/generous ¾ cup water
juice of 2 pink grapefruit
500ml/18fl oz/generous 2 cups sparkling water

Preparation
Pour the caster sugar and 200ml/7fl oz/ generous ¾ cup water into a jug. Let the sugar dissolve and then add the grapefruit juice.
    When you are ready to serve, add the sparkling water.
    Serve with plenty of ice.

... TEENAGE TIPS

Teenagers are universally always hungry, but you don't want to be cooking at all hours. These suggestions are all quick and delicious solutions to impromptu tummy rumblings.

My 3 Top Teenage Tips

* Sausages: If you are using the oven, cook some chipolatas alongside whatever else you're cooking. Just throw them into an oven dish, pour some clear honey over them and then bake until golden brown. They are irresistible and really useful if one of the kids arrives back from the beach starving. I guarantee they will all be eaten by the end of the day!

* The fish finger sandwich: Keep a little packet of fish fingers in your tiny freezer compartment – you never know when you're going to need them!

* Quick pizzas: If the weather is not so good, a fun thing to do at lunchtime is to get some mini pizza bases and let the children make their own pizzas in the caravan. Chopping, grating and deciding their own topping keeps them occupied on a rainy day – and you've sorted out lunch.

really quick fizzy elderflower

Homemade lemonade is wonderful, but sometimes you don't have the time or the inclination to make it. Here is a quick, refreshing drink that has a special occasion feel to it.

3–4 mint leaves
elderflower cordial
sparkling water
ice cubes

Preparation
Slice the mint leaves lengthwise into little strips.
Fill a large jug one-third full of ice cubes. Then pour in the cordial – the amount that suites your taste; my kids like it really strong. Fill the jug to the top with sparkling water and sprinkle in the mint leaves.
Serve immediately.

rice krispie cakes

This recipe makes a nice sticky cake that has a lovely shine to it. If you just melt chocolate you get a dull coating, but with this recipe they literally gleam.

I make a batch of these every couple of days when we're on holiday. Last summer, my son Dan would wake the entire family – arriving back from a night out, banging the caravan door and stating that he was starving and searching through the cupboards for something to eat. Desperate for a good night's sleep, I took to leaving a little Tupperware of these cakes out for him. It did the trick! They are perfect for picnics too.

100g/3^1/2oz/scant 1 stick butter
2 tbsp golden syrup
2 tbsp cocoa
100g/3^1/2oz/generous 3^1/2 cups rice krispies

Preparation
Butter a flat baking dish.

   Melt the butter in a large saucepan and add the syrup and cocoa. Once the mixture has bubbled for 1–2 minutes, take off the heat and pour in the cereals; mix until it is all covered in chocolate. Tip the mixture out onto your baking tray and spread out evenly, patting the mixture with the back of a wooden spoon. The mixture will take about 30 minutes to set, or about 15 minutes in the fridge, then you can cut it into squares.

pommes d'amour

I used to love toffee apples as a child. When I first made them for my children, they were nervous of biting into them. Now these are a regular on the Rivron menu. I take a serrated knife and I slice one up for me and Rowland; we are too fearful of loosing our teeth to actually eat one whole.

Preparation

Wash and dry the apples and hammer the lolly sticks into the apples. Butter a baking tray to put the apples onto when they have been toffeed.

Put the sugar, butter, vinegar, water and golden syrup in a pan and slowly dissolve the sugar, then bring to the boil and let it bubble furiously for about 6 minutes. You will see when the toffee is ready because it will suddenly change colour to a dark brown.

Take one apple at a time and gently swirl it around in the pan for 10 seconds. Transfer to the baking tray and leave to cool. Make sure the tray is right next to the hob, so as not to create trails of toffee.

Makes 6

6 Cox's apples (or any small, tart apple)
wooden lolly sticks
225g/8oz/1⅛ cups golden granulated or demerara sugar
2 tbsp butter
1 tsp malt vinegar
5 tbsp water
1 tbsp golden syrup

chicken crunch

This one is a real winner with our kids. If Rowland and I are eating at the campsite restaurant, I always make this for them. They don't like too much spice, but you can add more if you wish.

Serves 4
4 large chicken breasts, skinned and boned
2 egg
1 tsp ground turmeric
1 tsp ground cumin
1 tsp ground coriander
1/2 tsp chilli powder
2 tsp sugar
4 big handfuls cornflakes
4 tbsp plain flour
pinch salt
olive oil, for frying

Preparation
Slice each chicken breast into 4 or 5 thin strips. Beat the egg in a dish. Put the remaining ingredients into a second big dish, crushing the cornflakes with the back of a spoon until they are quite fine. Shake the dish so that the ingredients all mix in.

Put the chicken strips in the flour mixture and make sure each strip has a covering of flour. Dip each strip into the egg dish to coat, then put them back into the flour mixture for a second coating.

In a skillet pan or frying pan, heat the olive oil and when it is sizzling turn down the heat and place the chicken in the pan and cook for about 3 minutes on one side. Turn over to cook the other side, then turn again to prevent burning. The cooking time really depends of the thickness of the chicken; just check the middle of one of the fatter strips to make sure they are cooked through.

Serve with ketchup.

5. PUDDINGS AND BAKING

When we're caravanning, I often buy local delicacies for puddings, especially if we're in France and near a good patisserie. On the Isle of Wight, I buy Minghella's ice cream. And, of course, you can't beat strawberries and cream: I serve them after they've been sitting in 2 tablespoons of caster sugar for a couple of hours – this produces the most delicious syrup, which you can then spoon over like a sauce.

But there are some days when nothing but a home-made pudding will do. The recipes here are all quick and easy to prepare puddings that don't need fridge space. We all love the Night Light Melt (page 141) and are often found long after midnight still sitting around the table with only the light of the melting pot.

crêpes

Here is a basic recipe for crêpes, which are wonderfully wonderfully versatile. Our favourite toppings are the obvious ones: Nutella; ice cream; lemon and sugar; and golden syrup. We also enjoy bacon and banana; Maltesers; and hot sugared pineapple.

Makes 6
4 eggs
140g/5oz/scant 1 cup plain flour
250ml/8fl oz/1 cup milk
pinch salt
butter, for frying

Preparation
Put the ingredients into the blender in this order: eggs, flour, milk, then salt. This stops the flour sticking to the bottom. Blend together. Allowing the mixture to stand for 30 minutes will improve the texture, but sometimes you just can't wait!

Melt a little butter in a frying pan, pour in $^1/_6$ of the mixture, then fry each crêpe until golden.

Serve immediately.

Sometimes there is only one pudding that will do: apple crumble with custard. Here is a recipe with very little baking time but all the flavour and comfort of a traditional crumble.

This can be prepared ahead of time, and then baked just before serving.

caravan crumble

Serves 4
6 apples
200g/7oz Nice biscuits
100ml/3^{1}/2fl oz/scant ^{1}/2 cup water
100g/3^{1}/2oz /^{1}/2 cup soft brown sugar
100g/3^{1}/2oz/^{7}/8 stick butter

Preparation
Preheat the oven to 200°C/400°F/Gas mark 7.

Peel and cut the apples into large chunks (about the size of tinned pineapple chunks). Empty the Nice biscuits into a bowl and crush with the end of the rolling pin to achieve a breadcrumb texture.

Have ready a sieve over a bowl. Put the apples in a pan with the water, sugar and butter and bring to boiling point, then simmer gently for about 6 minutes. You want the apples to be cooked but still remain firm. Strain the apple and juice from the pan through a sieve. Pour the liquid back into the pan and boil for 5 minutes and put the apples into your crumble dish. The liquid will reduce and become a lovely syrup; when it's ready, pour it over the apple. Cover the apple with the crushed biscuit.

Pop the crumble into the oven for 10 minutes.

Serve with custard or vanilla ice cream.

strawberry swirl

These are so sweet, and look like something you would buy in a French patisserie. One packet of pastry makes five or six little pastries, depending on the size you want.

Serves 4
375g/13oz puff pastry
200g/7oz punnet strawberries, cut into quarters
200g/7oz punnet blueberries
butter
soft brown sugar
1 egg, beaten

Preparation

Preheat the oven to 180°C/350°F/Gas mark 4.

Roll out the pastry to the thickness of a 50 pence piece. Cut into circles 17cm/8in in diameter – I cut round my small mixing bowl.

Put a little pile of strawberries and 5–6 blueberries in the middle of the pastry, then put a knob of butter on top and 1 teaspoon of sugar. Paint the rest of the pastry that you can see to the edge with beaten egg. Gather the whole circle of pastry and make a little pouch, then twist to seal. Paint the outside with beaten egg and sprinkle with sugar. Bake for 15 minutes.

Serve with a scoop of vanilla ice cream.

grape brûlée

This brûlée is an old favourite of mine, and everyone is so impressed by it that I am almost embarrassed to tell you how easy it is to make. It is light and refreshing, because I replace the cream with Greek yogurt, which offers a lovely combination of sweet and tart.

Serves 4
100g/3$\frac{1}{2}$oz/$\frac{1}{2}$ cup seedless green grapes, cut in half
500g/1lb 2oz/2$\frac{1}{4}$ cups Greek yogurt
75g/2$\frac{3}{4}$ oz/generous $\frac{1}{3}$ cup white granulated sugar
75g/2$\frac{3}{4}$ oz/generous $\frac{1}{3}$ cup soft brown sugar

Preparation
Put the grapes in a small ovenproof dish and spread the Greek yogurt on top. Cover with clingfilm and leave in the fridge. You can do this earlier in the day if you like.

When you are ready to serve the brûlée, turn on the grill to high, making sure you take the grill pan out. Mix the two sugars together and completely cover the yogurt with the sugars. Put the dish under the grill: the sugar will caramelize very quickly and turn a golden brown and then go hard. This should take no more than 5 minutes. Serve immediately!

honeycomb pudding with lemon cream

This is the most delicious pudding. It is so light and incredibly easy to make. It does look a little like a pudding from the 1970s, but you are in a caravan after all!

The Lemon Cream is also wonderful on meringues or fresh fruit.

Serves 4
300ml/10fl oz/1¹/₄ cups double cream
150g/5¹/₂oz honeycomb or 4 Crunchie Bars
100g/3¹/₂oz/¹/₂ cup granulated sugar
juice of 1 lemon
100ml/3¹/₂fl oz/scant ¹/₂ cup water

Preparation
Whisk the double cream till it is thick and peaky. Put the Crunchie bars in a freezer bag and bash them with a rolling pin to break them into little bits.
   For the lemon cream, put the sugar, lemon juice and water in a saucepan and bring to the boil. When the sugar is dissolved and it starts looking syrup-like, take off the heat. You don't want to caramelise the sugar. Mix the syrup in with the whisked cream. Then put your crushed Crunchie bars into 4 wine glasses and put your lemon cream on top.

miniature lemon drizzle cakes

These are so sweet; they are like little lemon puddings.

Makes 12
150g/5^1/2oz/scant ^{3}/4 cup butter
150g/5^1/2oz/^{3}/4 cup caster sugar
3 eggs
150g/5^1/2oz/1 cup self-raising flour, sifted
1 tsp lemon zest
Topping
100g/3^1/2oz /3^1/2oz/^{1}/2 cup caster sugar
juice of 3 lemons

Preparation
Preheat the oven to 180°C/350°F/Gas mark 4. Line your fairy cake tin with paper cases (unless it is silicone). For the topping, put the sugar and lemon juice in a jam jar and shake until all the sugar is dissolved.

In a large mixing bowl, cream the butter and the sugar. Add the eggs with a little of the flour to avoid curdling. Fold in the rest of the flour and the lemon zest.

Pop the cake mixture into your fairy cake tins and bake for 20 minutes. When you take them out of the oven, pierce them with a skewer – about 6 times on each cake – then spoon over some of the topping from the jar. Leave them in the tin until they cool. The sugar will crystallize on the top and the lemon will seep into the cake.

Serve with Yogurt Cream (page 139) or Lemon Cream (page 135).

sugared oranges

This is a fantastically easy dessert to put together, and the warm orange goes beautifully with cold Yogurt Cream (opposite).

Serves 4
4 oranges
50g/1³/₄oz/scant ¹/₄ cup butter
50g/1³/₄oz/¹/₄ cup granulated sugar
pinch mixed spice

Preparation
Slice the oranges around the equator. You won't be able to use the end pieces. Take off as much of the skin and white pith as you can without losing the shape of the orange.

In your frying-pan, melt the butter and then with a wooden spoon stir in the sugar and mixed spice. When the sugar has dissolved, add the slices of orange. Pan-fry the orange for about two minutes each side. Place of a plate and spoon over the lovely warm spicy buttery syrup.

Serve with Yogurt Cream (opposite).

This is lovely light alternative to cream and it is almost a dessert in itself.

yogurt cream

200ml/7fl oz/generous $^3/_4$ cup double cream
200ml/7fl oz/generous $^3/_4$ cup Greek yogurt
2 tbsp icing sugar

Preparation
Whisk the double cream until thick and then add the Greek yogurt and icing sugar. Cover and leave in the fridge until needed.

night light melt

This is such a lovely way to spend an evening, and we came across it by accident. We were in a beautiful cooking shop when my daughter spotted a sweet little ceramic bowl on a stand, with a night light underneath for gently heating its contents – our very own mini fondue kit, complete with little forks. I bought some chocolate and strawberries and that evening, after supper, we all sat around gorging ourselves on fresh strawberries and delicious melted chocolate. That summer, we were browsing in a kitchen shop in France and found a similar kit. This time, I bought loads of chocolate and lots of different fruits and now we are often found sitting around the table long into the night, dipping an array of fruits into our chocolate fondue.

Preparation
All you have to do is get some good-quality chocolate and fruit. Chop the fruit into little chunks and break up the chocolate into the bowl, then light the night-light. We all have our favourites: Ned likes grapes; Ella loves strawberries; Dan goes for tangerine, Rowland prefers pineapple – and I just like them all.

Be warned: this is irresistible to kids of all ages!

... RAINY DAY BAKING

I love rainy day baking. I have put in two recipes for bread because a caravan is the perfect place to make bread – when you have done your kneading, you can prove the bread really easily in your warm cosy caravan. I had to put in a recipe for scones because you're on holiday, so you deserve at least one cream tea! Baking is also a great way to entertain the kids when it's too wet to go outside. (And a way of making treats for a picnic when the weather does improve!)

chocolate dreams

I am always making Chocolate Dreams. If any of the children have a friend round, I'll automatically makes some. They are fantastic for picnics, make a great snack if small tummies are rumbling and it's hours till the next meal, and are delicious with a cup of tea!

Makes 12
100g/3¹/₂oz/¹/₂ cup caster sugar
100g/3¹/₂oz/ ⁷/₈ stick butter
2 eggs, beaten
100g/3¹/₂oz/²/₃ cup self-raising flour, sifted
2 tbsp cocoa
150g/5¹/₂oz/scant 1 cup milk chocolate chips

Preparation
Preheat the oven to 180°C/350°F/Gas mark 4. Line your fairy cake tin with paper cases (unless it is silicone).

Cream the sugar and the butter until smooth and creamy. Add the eggs with a little flour and mix with a wooden spoon, then add the rest of the flour and the cocoa and whisk very briefly. Finally, add the chocolate chips, mixing them in with a wooden spoon.

Spoon out into the fairy cake tin and bake for about 20 minutes. Check by gently pushing down in the middle: if they bounce back, they are cooked; if not, leave them a little longer. If you are making these in a silicone tin, leave for about 10 minutes, then transfer to a cooling tray. If you are using a traditional tin, transfer to a cooling tray immediately.

chocolate brownies

A camp is not a camp without chocolate brownies! They keep for a few days and are ideal for picnics.

125g/4¹/₂oz/4¹/₂ squares plain chocolate, broken into pieces
125g/4¹/₂oz/1¹/₈ sticks butter
225g/8oz/1¹/₈ cups caster sugar
2 eggs
125g/4¹/₂oz/generous ³/₄ cup plain flour
¹/₂ tsp baking powder
125g/4¹/₂oz/1¹/₈ cups walnuts, chopped

Preparation

Preheat the oven to 180°C/350°F/Gas mark 4. Grease a shallow 28 x 18cm (11 x 7in) rectangular tin.

Put the chocolate and butter in a mixing bowl and put the bowl over a saucepan of gently bubbling water. When the butter and chocolate have melted, take off the heat and stir in all the remaining ingredients. Pour into your tin and spread it out.

Bake for 30 minutes. Take them out of the oven and leave in the tin for 10 minutes, then cut them into squares and put out on a cooling tray.

extremely light chocolate cake

This cake really is extremely light and has the appearance of a sophisticated gâteau. It is so fantastic to make a chocolate cake in the caravan – and so rewarding. The down side is there is quite a lot of washing up, but hey, it's worth it.

A small tub of Greek yogurt is 150g/5¹/₂oz, so use 1 tablespoon in the cake, and the rest for the filling.

Preparation

Preheat your oven to 180°C/350°F/Gas mark 4. Grease your cake tin (if it is not a silicone one).

Cream the butter and sugar. Add the eggs with a spoonful of flour, so as not to curdle the mixture and whisk for another minute. Fold in the rest of the flour and cocoa, then add the Greek yogurt and whisk to loosen the density of the mixture. Pour into the tin and pop in the oven for 25–30 minutes.

When the cake is cool, make the filling. Whisk the double cream, yogurt, icing sugar and cocoa all together all together until the cream thickens, taking care to stop before it clots. You have just made the most delicious topping.

Slice the cake in half and fill the middle with half of the chocolate cream, then sandwich the cake together. Cover the top of the cake with the remaining mixture.

Dust the top with icing sugar, then serve.

150g/5¹/₂oz/scant ³/₄ cup butter, plus extra
    for greasing
150g/5¹/₂oz/³/₄ cup caster sugar
3 eggs, beaten
150g/5¹/₂oz/1 cup self-raising flour, sifted
2 heaped tbsp cocoa
1 heaped tbsp Greek yogurt

Filling and Topping
200ml/7fl oz/generous ³/₄ cup double cream
120g/4¹/₄oz/generous ¹/₂ cup Greek yogurt
100g/3¹/₂oz/1 cup icing sugar, plus extra for
    dusting
2 heaped tbsp cocoa

flapjack

Flapjacks are fantastic for taking on a picnic, easy to pack away in a little Tupperware box. If they get a little warm in the picnic bag, they will just taste better ...

My daughter Ella is our resident flapjack maker!

125g/4^1/$_2$oz/1^1/$_8$ sticks butter
50g/1^3/$_4$oz/^{1}/$_4$ cup demerara sugar
1 tbsp golden syrup
225g/8oz/3 cups porridge oats

Preparation

Grease a 28 x 18cm (11 x 7in) rectangular tin. Preheat the oven to 180°C/350°F/Gas mark 4.

Put the butter, sugar and syrup in a saucepan. Melt them over a low heat and stir with a wooden spoon. Take the pan off the heat and add the oats, then stir well. Pour the mixture into the tin and press down, then bake for 20 minutes. Take out of the oven and carefully cut the flapjack into squares, then leave to cool. Lift them out of the tin and store in an airtight container.

fudge

There is something about fudge … We eat it only when we're on holiday.
It's so easy to make and it's great to take on a picnic or to just indulge with
a coffee after lunch. Also if you are going to visit friends when on holiday it's
a lovely little gift to bring.

450g/1lb/2¼ cups soft brown sugar
50g/1¾oz/scant ¼ cup butter
275ml/9fl oz/scant 1¼ cups milk
a few drops of vanilla essence

Preparation
Grease a small baking tray.
 Heat the sugar, butter and milk in a saucepan until the sugar melts,
stirring all the time. Bring it to the boil, and then let it boil for 30 minutes.
Test to see if it is ready by dropping a little fudge into a bowl of cold water;
it should form a soft ball. If not, boil it a little more and test again.
 Take of the heat and beat in the vanilla essence until the mixture is thick
and creamy, then pour into the tin and leave to set. Cut with a knife into
small squares.

focaccia

Focaccia is a lovely Italian bread that just speaks summer time. It is really easy to make and goes so well with salad.

2 tsp dried yeast
500g/1lb 2oz/3¹/₃ cups strong white bread flour, sifted
1 tsp salt
90ml/3fl oz/¹/₃ cup olive oil, plus extra for greasing
300ml/10fl oz/1¹/₄ cups warm water
coarse sea salt for sprinkling
1 sprig rosemary, chopped into small pieces

Preparation
Paint a baking tray with oil. Preheat the oven to 220°C/425°F/Gas mark 7.

Stir the yeast into the flour, add the teaspoon of salt and then 4 tablespoons olive oil and mix until it resembles breadcrumbs. Make a well and add the water and mix; it will look sticky.

Flour your hands and the cooking area; scoop the dough out of the bowl and onto the flour counter. Kneed until the dough is smooth. Clear out the remaining flour bits from the bowl, then wipe the sides with a small amount of oil and put the dough back in the bowl. Cover with clingfilm and leave to rise in a warm area. (I think next to the hot water tank is perfect, or if you've had the heating on, the wardrobe.) If you are putting it by direct sunlight, cover the bowl with a clean damp tea towel to avoid getting a hard crust on the top. It needs to double in size, which should take about 45 minutes.

Gently place the dough back onto your floured surface. Knead the dough again; this is called knocking back. Then roll the dough into a circular shape. Using your finger, make little indentations at intervals. Pour 2 tablespoons of olive oil over the bread and liberally sprinkle with sea salt and the rosemary bits.

Bake in the oven for 5 minutes at 220°C/425°F/Gas mark 7, then reduce the temperature to 200°C/400°F/Gas mark 6 for a further 10 minutes.

Serve warm or cold.

bread

A caravan is the perfect place to make bread and I don't think there is anything more satisfying to cook. When the bread comes out of the oven, the sense of achievement is wonderful. Children love bread making – I think because the kneading and shaping makes it so hands-on. Here is a very simple recipe, which the whole family will enjoy. This recipe will make about 10 bread rolls.

600g/1lb 5oz/4 cups strong white bread flour
pinch salt
15g/^{1}/$_2$oz quick yeast
400ml/14fl oz/scant 1^3/$_4$ cups warm (not hot) water
100ml/3^1/$_2$fl oz/scant ^{1}/$_2$ cup olive oil, plus extra for greasing

Preparation

Grease a baking tray with a small amount of olive oil.

Put the flour in a large mixing bowl with the salt and the yeast. Make a well in the centre of the flour and then pour in the water and olive oil. Mix with all your might, till it looks sticky.

Flour your hands and then scoop up the dough in one ball, and put it onto a floured surface. Start kneading until it feels soft and smooth, about 5 minutes; the stronger you knead, the softer the bread. Put the dough back into your mixing bowl, and cover with clingfilm and then put in a warm place for the dough to rise. (I think my cupboard above the heater is a perfect place, and near the hot water tank under the sofa is another good place, but anywhere nice and warm will do.)

Preheat the oven to 220°C/425°F/Gas mark 7. When the dough has doubled in size, flour your hands and scoop it out of the bowl onto a floured surface and gently knead for about 30 seconds; this is called knocking back.

Shape the dough; bread rolls are fun to shape and they take no time to cook. Depending on the size of your rolls, they should take about 15 minutes in the oven. You will be able to tell when they are cooked by their colour. If you're not sure, pick one up and knock the bottom; it should sound hollow.

Leave on a cooling tray and serve warm.

scones

I am sure you all know how to make scones, but there is something about a cream tea when you are on holiday – especially if you are staying somewhere they have local clotted cream.

225g/8oz/1½ cups self-raising flour
pinch salt
1 tsp baking powder
3 tbsp butter
150ml/5fl oz/ ⅔ cup milk
1 egg, beaten, to glaze

Preparation

Preheat the oven to 220°C/425°F/Gas mark 7. Grease your baking sheet.

Sift the flour, adding the salt and baking powder. Rub the butter into the flour until it looks and feels like fine breadcrumbs, then pour in the milk carefully so the mixture is a soft dough and dry enough to roll out.

Flour your surface and the rolling pin and roll out the dough so it is about 2cm/¾in thick. Cut into rounds using a 6cm/2½in round pastry cutter cut, then place on the baking tray. Brush with the beaten egg and bake for about 10 minutes, until they are a light golden colour. Cool slightly on a baking tray, then serve: they are most delicious when still warm.

chocolate chip cookies

Our kids love these cookies, and so do all their friends. Rarely a day goes by without me making a batch. These taste even better when they have been cooked in the caravan.

You should have two shelves in your oven, so you will be able to cook two trays at a time. This recipe makes 15 large cookies, 5 on each baking tray. I suggest you cook two trays together, and as soon as one tray is free, cook the third batch. Or, if you are a small party, put half the cookie dough in a plastic bag in the fridge and cook a second batch a few days later.

125g/4^1/2oz/1^1/8 sticks butter
150g/5^1/2oz/1^3/4 cups granulated sugar
1 egg, beaten
150g/5^1/2oz/1 cup wholemeal flour, sifted
150g/5^1/2oz/scant 1 cup chocolate chips
1 tsp bicarbonate of soda

Preparation
Preheat the oven to 200°C/400°F/Gas mark 6.
  Cream the butter and sugar. Add the egg, flour, chocolate chips and bicarbonate of soda, and beat as hard as you can; it's a bit tough going at the beginning but it soon mixes in. Roll the dough into satsuma-sized balls place on the tray and then flatten slightly with the palm of your hand.
  Bake in the oven for 12 minutes. When you take them out, loosen with a pallet knife but leave on the tray for a further 3 minutes, then transfer to a cooling tray.

index

acknowledgements

I would like to thank Anna Cheifetz at Pavilion, Nikki Nichol at the Caravan Club, Simon and Nick Howard at Bailey Caravans, Wei and Yuki for the beautiful pictures and Georgie for the wonderful design. I would also like to thank my fabulous girlfriends, Elisa Anniss, Ellie Gliksten and Charlotte Hudson, for their invaluable support; my lovely children Dan, Ella and Ned, without whom we would never have had so many brilliant caravan adventures, and lastly my wonderful husband Rowland who has encouraged me all the way.

First published in paperback in the United Kingdom in 2019 by
Pavilion Books
43 Great Ormond Street
London WC1N 3HZ

ISBN: 978-1-911624-71-4

A CIP catalogue record for this book is available from the British Library

10 9 8 7 6 5 4 3 2 1

Reproduction by Rival Colour Ltd, UK
Printed and bound by Toppan Leefung Printing Ltd, China

www.pavilionbooks.com

MIX
Paper from
responsible sources
FSC® C104723